Praise for *Pushed*

D1534064

N USA winner
)f *Stars Go Blue*

"The records are scant and the stories contradictory, but Spagna embraces the ambiguities of her adventure. What she finds is not so much the definitive truth of this history, but rather the deep stories behind Chinese exclusion, Indian campaigns, and Manifest Destiny, an emotional terrain that undergirds the xenophobia of our times."

—TEOW LIM GOH, author of *Islanders*

"*Pushed* grounds us in a landscape, and then explores—in vivid detail through the eyes and heart of a compassionate and curious narrator—what the land holds: the history, the questions, the bridge of shared references, and the silences. Spagna masterfully lets the reader experience an unfolding mystery alongside her, providing an in-depth snapshot of a particular place she loves in Washington State that holds a complex historical conflict, as she turns and turns the story to trouble the nature of 'truth' and ask what remains."

—SONYA HUBER, author of *Supremely Tiny Acts:*
A Memoir of a Day

"Spagna takes us sleuthing to uncover the facts surrounding the story of hundreds of Chinese miners being killed in late 1800s Chelan, Washington. We read of her adventurous traveling for interviews, examining microfilm, finding newspapers, looking at survey maps, and there is even grave dowsing as we are brought yet closer through artful speculation to the more complex truth of massacres and the xenophobic history of the Pacific Northwest. Spagna crafts this investigation with great care; all of this becomes a recounting of the highest order."

—ALLEN GEE, author of *My Chinese-America*

"Spagna brings a storyteller's gifts to bear in unearthing the truth of a tragic event mostly forgotten…if it happened at all. The specifics of who did what and when aren't even all that important;

what is important is that, so typical to the 'heroic' narrative of the West, the larger story relates to the treatment of a people most western mythmakers would prefer we forget, prefer we not engage with and rectify. *Pushed* is Spagna's heart-full effort in making certain this injustice will not be overlooked."

—CHRIS LA TRAY, author of *One-Sentence Journal*

PUSHED

PUSHED

MINERS, A MERCHANT, AND (MAYBE) A MASSACRE

Ana Maria Spagna

TORREY HOUSE PRESS

Salt Lake City • Torrey

First Torrey House Press Edition, February 2023
Copyright © 2023 by Ana Maria Spagna

Published by Torrey House Press
Salt Lake City, Utah
www.torreyhouse.org

International Standard Book Number: 978-1-948814-69-0
E-book ISBN: 978-1-948814-70-6
Library of Congress Control Number: 2021952947

Cover design by Kathleen Metcalf
Interior design by Rachel Buck-Cockayne
Distributed to the trade by Consortium Book Sales and Distribution

Torrey House Press offices in Salt Lake City sit on the homelands of Ute, Goshute, Shoshone, and Paiute nations. Offices in Torrey are on the homelands of Southern Paiute, Ute, and Navajo nations.

Table of Contents

PART III: WHAT IF?

Notes on terminology

At the time when the Chelan Falls Massacre (may have) occurred, Indigenous people in the American West were referred to as "Indians," a misguided moniker and a particularly stubborn remnant of colonialism. When quoting historical sources, I've left the word in place. In contemporary cases, with the generous input of members of the Federated Tribes of the Colville Reservation and others, I've used specific labels preferred by local Indigenous peoples and/or individuals (e.g. the Chelan and Entiat Tribes, the Osoyoos Indian Band). When speaking in my own voice, and/or in more general terms, I've turned for guidance to *Elements of Indigenous Style: A Guide for Writing By and About Indigenous Peoples* by Gregory Younging. I apologize in advance for any missteps, and I welcome dialogue.

The word *Okanogan*, a place name, is spelled with an *o* in the United States, but confusingly with an *a* in Canada, *Okanagan*. The Indigenous nation also spells the name *Okanagan*.

Prologue

Ten miles from the head of Lake Chelan—the "landing" as we call what passes for town—a high bridge spans the Stehekin River where it charges through a narrow gorge of lichen-stained gneiss. Firs and ferns root in tiny crevices of vertical rock. On a hot July day, pre-run, I stand on the bridge watching the blue-green churn, the roiling waves. We're in a strange season, mid-pandemic—time is compressed and urgent at once—and the temperature today is predicted to top 105 degrees. Twigs and cones snap underfoot, so wildfires can't be far off, but somehow, right here, right now, it's possible to feel removed. If you kick the dust and focus your eyes, you can find shards of obsidian from hundreds of miles away, evidence of Interior and Coast Salish people who've trekked these mountains for thousands of years. A cool morning breeze lifts off the snowmelt water. Dogwood and cedar limbs bob lazily. Death counts mount.

I've always said I want my ashes scattered here. This is where my wife, Laurie, and I met some thirty years ago when we lived as roommates in the historic ranger cabin under the pines where the roar of the river lulled us to sleep. We had no running water, no electricity, but plenty of wine and Van Morrison on cassette. We eventually built our own home five miles down the road, and we still drive or ski or walk this dirt road regularly to gaze down at the midstream boulder that disappears in floodwater and protrudes during drought. In fall, kokanee salmon spawn orange,

1

a carpet in the eddy. In winter snow pillows pile high. I like to think my ashes will wash up one day on the icy banks of the river, clotted on rocks with rotted fish and cedar drift, or maybe travel farther to the deep cold lake and on to the once-mighty Columbia, slowed by dams and polluted by quicksilver and plutonium, rich with sturgeon and lamprey, osprey and cranes. And history.

Some people have a passion for genealogy, and I get it. I've seen traces in myself of ancestors I never, or barely, knew: my archbishop great-uncle, a cerebral diplomat, my Italian great-grandparents with meaty dirt-callused palms, my Irish grandmother with an easy wide-mouthed laugh who played a mean game of Scrabble. My people were earnest newcomers, careless encroachers, faithful believers in a murderous faith, writers of words, singers of songs, builders of buildings, ambitious vulnerable misguided energetic stubborn sad joyous humans. I recognize them in the mirror, and I'm grateful to them. Still, I've never felt a strong desire to retrace their steps.

My attention, which sometimes leans closer to devotion, has always turned to the land. For a long time, I nurtured it by moving farther and farther from other people, toward wilderness and the transcendence that books promised I'd find there. Or maybe that's not right. Maybe it wasn't books so much, or anything as ethereal as transcendence. When I walked alone on an unnamed ridge cloaked in red heather, or skied through the silent forest after new snow, I felt a visceral tug sure as caffeine coursing after coffee or euphoria after exercise or the heart-softened gush when you look in a newborn's eyes, something physically undeniable. For many years I worked as a seasonal laborer, maintaining hiking trails in the backcountry, ten hours a day with hand tools. Just to be *out there*. Eventually, I fell in love, bought land, and built a cabin. Even when I did, I didn't like to say I owned land. Instead, I'd say something like this: There's a way a place comes to own you.

To talk about this region, you need a mental map.

Take a piece of paper, hold it sideways, and call it Washington State. Canada on top, Oregon below. Fold it in half. The Cascade Mountains run vertically down the page just left of center and block clouds from moving east, so the famous forest-green cities—Seattle, Tacoma, Olympia—crowd the left side. Eastern Washington is on the right: wide and dry, farmland and small towns, low shrubs and sagebrush.

From the top right-hand corner, the Columbia River leaves Canada and runs diagonally across Eastern Washington. If you follow the river down and stop about one third of the way— smack in the middle of the state—you'll see a long skinny lake, Lake Chelan, its name derived from the Wenatchi: *Tsi-Laan* for "deep water." (It's a natural lake, yes, but dammed, too. A small-ish hydroelectric dam built in the 1920s raises the water level some twenty feet in summer.) Glacier-carved and fjord-like, the lake stretches fifty-five miles toward the wet-dry divide.

Stehekin, my longtime home at the north end, is remote and densely forested. The name, from American Salishan, is often interpreted as "the way through" but more accurately translates as "trail's end." Accessible only by foot or ferry, the tiny mountain village is home to eighty or so year-round residents including Laurie and me.

Chelan, at the south end, is a tourist mecca. Pink-skinned visitors flock there from growth-sick Seattle to soak in the sun. Chelan was once known mainly for apples. Cold winters, hot dry summers, and rich volcanic soil combined to make the apples sweet and crisp. The orchards remain, but in recent years, they're often torn out and replaced with vineyards and adjacent wineries, which are more attractive to the many many tourists who lounge on floaty toys, rent Jet Skis, shop for sunscreen at Safeway, go wine tasting, water sliding, watch the sun drop, orange with smoke, over the blue blue lake.

Now. If you take a short steep curvy highway southward

down from Chelan, you reach the town of Chelan Falls. On an actual map, you may not find it. The town is super small, a dot or a speck at best—population of 186, now more than half Latino, mostly Mexican. The Columbia River at the town edge, thanks to Rocky Reach Dam thirty-five miles downstream, is flat and slow as bathwater. To confuse matters, there's no waterfall, none you can see. There are, however, apple orchards. Orchards, orchards, everywhere, along the river and atop wide-enough bluffs, patchwork strips and squares of irrigated green amid the brown. If you look directly across the Columbia from Chelan Falls, you see Beebe Bridge Park.

A few years ago, while waiting for the ferry to Stehekin, I browsed the shelves at Riverwalk Books, the fine independent bookstore in downtown Chelan, and picked up a thin paperback titled *Wapato Heritage: The History of the Chelan and Entiat Indians* by Tom Hackenmiller. Why? Because a new tugging had begun. Simple questions that may be easy enough to answer in some places, but are murkier here: Who came before us? What did they do? Who and what did they love? How did they experience red heather ridges or too-long winter nights? The people of the Chelan and Entiat bands, who lived along and traveled Lake Chelan for millennia, were largely displaced by the US government in the 1890s and moved to the Colville Reservation, one hundred miles east. Such recent history!

As I read and reread *Wapato Heritage*, another story snagged my attention. This one wasn't exactly about the original inhabitants—or not them alone. In the late 1860s, a Chinese merchant settled on the bank of the Columbia River directly across from Chelan Falls, where Beebe Bridge Park now sits. The merchant ran a thriving business, the first of its kind along this rugged upper stretch of river, and he catered to Indigenous, Chinese, and white people alike. But within a decade, tensions grew heated. One day on a high bluff within view of the store, according to lore, a group of Indigenous people murdered a large number of Chinese miners—perhaps as many as three hundred—and pushed the bodies over a cliff into the Columbia. Locals dubbed the event the Chelan Falls Massacre.

A *massacre*? Perhaps as many as *three hundred* killed?

Why had I never heard this story?

Truth is, I'd never even heard about Chinese gold miners along the Columbia, though I should have. I knew very little about Chinese people in the American West, though I've lived here my entire life, and later I'd learn about a bustling Chinatown in my hometown of Riverside, California. I also didn't know why Indigenous people would feel animosity toward the Chinese miners, though I could make a few guesses—innate distrust? prescient protectionism? sheer frustration? But I did know Beebe Bridge Park, a flat grassy campground constructed in the mid-1990s, managed by Chelan Public Utilities District and popular with RVers in summer. I'd often camped there on my way to or from the once-a-day ferry. Beebe Bridge had always seemed a nondescript in-between sort of place, alluring only for its proximity to water in this desert-dry region or, in my case, for its cheap clean showers. To think of Beebe Bridge as historically relevant felt surprising, astonishing even, a welcome challenge to assumptions I didn't know I'd held. This simple connection, at first, spurred the tugging.

Soon, other changes spurred me. The 2016 presidential election exposed xenophobia in the United States in ways too many of us had never imagined or at least wildly underestimated. Vehement rejection of immigrants raged everywhere. On Twitter, on cable news and in the streets, people cried, over and over, that this behavior was unprecedented. If nothing else, the story of the Chelan Falls Massacre belied that refrain. Unbridled hatred of strangers has always been with us. The new regime only rekindled the fire.

Around the same time, I took a temporary teaching job and moved for a year to Walla Walla, Washington, a small town four hours south of Lake Chelan, and by coincidence, another place where the Chinese merchant had spent time. In Walla Walla, I became, for a time, a stranger myself, and as such, I related in small ways with the merchant. Chinese people in the American West—from what, at first, I could glean—had been itinerant workers, short-timers, hand tool laborers. They came and they went. Then they disappeared. Where did they go? And why? As much as the massacre and the intentions of the attackers, I wanted to understand this Chinese merchant: the relationships he forged, where he went and why, and what legacy he left behind, if any.

The story grew more complicated. Not long after beginning research in earnest, I began to hear another theory about the Chelan Falls Massacre. First as a scandalous whisper: *You know what they say...* Then as a steady hum. Sons and daughters of the sons and daughters of the first white settlers voiced the possibility. A natural history of the Columbia River, *Native River* by William D. Layman, quoted a later merchant, Que Yu, saying the same thing: The attackers weren't Indigenous people. They were white men dressed up to look Indigenous.

The possibility infuriated me. Of course! Xenophobia isn't innate, but instilled, a political tool, an excuse. None of this was new. None of this could be substantiated. And because the facts remained so murky, I'd learn, some historians believed the massacre never occurred at all. Suddenly a made-up massacre seemed possible, too.

If a place comes to own you, does its history own you, too? I believe it does.

I've read a thousand pages and driven hundreds of miles trying to figure out the truth about this forgotten massacre. I used to think of forgetting as benign, such a gentle verb—to forget—a venial sin. Now I am not so sure. I own land in Chelan County. I've benefitted as much as anyone—and more than most—from the murders of non-white people. The sin of forgetting, venial or mortal, is at least partly mine. I didn't always think this way. Maybe moving away changed my perspective. Or maybe middle age did. Certainly, I've gained a broader understanding of history thanks to good historians and, ironically enough, to bad politicians.

So, call this remembering. A search with no end. A river with multiple sloughs.

A group of Indigenous people massacred a few Chinese men.

Or three hundred of them.

Or white men massacred them.

Or it didn't happen at all.

Tributaries trickle and flood and sometimes run dry. Who believes which story and why? Why tell the story at all?

"Every hillside, every valley, every plain and grove, has been hallowed by some sad or happy event in days long vanished," Chief Si'ahl famously said, or may have said, in 1854 in response to a proposed treaty that effectively stole a large chunk of his homeland including the city of Seattle. The veracity of the transcript, which only appeared several years after the speech, has been fiercely debated in a way that would become eerily familiar to me as I sussed out this massacre story. "Even the rocks, which seem to be dumb and dead as they swelter in the sun along the silent shore, thrill with memories of stirring events…" It's a perspective we colonizers either romanticize or dismiss but rarely acknowledge as plain fact. Or plain lack. We've lost the sense of comfort and complicity such connection can spawn, and maybe one way to nurture understanding, to suture some semblance of wholeness, is to unbury stories of what humans did.

Right here.

PART I:
OVER THE EDGE

Chapter One
MASSACRE: VERSION I

The attackers approach with stealth from three sides. Wind blows fierce and steady, omnipresent. Tawny hills stretch and roll, taut as muscles on a cougar's back, toward the blue horizon—picture the painted backdrop for a western—and obscure the gorge, a long cliff-drop to the river below. The attackers carry weapons, but they'll hardly need them. As soon as the miners appear—sinewy men, beardless as boys, baggy shirts billowing in the hot wind, the incessant infuriating wind—they're herded to the edge.

A howling horrid death. Deaths, plural.

Close to midnight on Halloween at a neighbor's Stehekin cabin, I stood dressed in a heavy leopard-print cloak and a ratty borrowed wig—a theme-free costume somewhere between a wildcat and Pebbles Flintstone—when I started asking around. The ragtag crowd was medium-drunk and medium-loud, picking at the last of the hors d'oeuvres, ignoring a dance mix on repeat. Why start talking massacre? Maybe it was the point in the evening where you'll talk about anything, or maybe, when I saw Dave Clouse across the room, I remembered seeing his name on a list of volunteers for the Chelan Historical Society. Dave was dressed as a logger redneck, and his wife, Sue, a retired high school art teacher, was dressed as a hippie, exaggerations of who

11

they once were, who we all were, back in the day. He was holding a PBR as a prop while I was drinking one for real.

The Chelan Falls Massacre? Yeah, yeah, he said. We've heard of it.

I was shocked.

For a few months, I'd been poring over the same information—or lack thereof—repeated in small-print-run histories, small-town museum exhibits, coffee table books, and dense-text websites, and I'd found little. I'd consulted historians, pondered motives, and scanned road cuts on highway drives between Chelan and Wenatchee, the bigger town where Laurie and I buy groceries about once a month when we take the ferry downlake. As I drove the familiar stretch and listened to radio commentators discuss the upcoming election and one candidate's so-called crisis of immigration, the fact that little information exists about this 1875 massacre of Chinese people along the Columbia River, right here, very nearly in our own backyard, began to feel less like a curiosity and more like an outrage. No one had seemed to know much. No one had seemed to care. Until Dave and Sue.

Do you know where the massacre took place, exactly? I asked Dave.

He didn't, but he'd always wondered, and Sue knew some stories. They were game for sleuthing. Winter would arrive soon, but we decided, come spring, we'd take a drive to see if we could find the spot.

And so, come March 2017, as the country roiled in transition, Dave, Sue, and I met in Chelan and piled into their Subaru. We followed an unmarked but well-maintained gravel road out of town. This was, they explained, an old stagecoach road, the original route from Chelan to Chelan Falls—from the shores of Lake Chelan to the banks of the Columbia—and it took us past an old dump and several ramshackle trailers, loosely following the Chelan River gorge. The hills were winter brown, the peaks on the horizon white with snow, the sky blue, the air warm. Dave drove, and Sue shared the backseat with their dog, Daisy, while I rode shotgun and scanned the horizon.

The Chelan River drops fast and steep, like a spigot draining the lake, the rocky gorge narrow as a gash. Even from the gravel road near the edge, we couldn't see water. Across the gorge, atop the rolling bluffs, we could see brand-new fruit-packing warehouses built in the wake of wildfires and desert shrubs blooming yellow. If it rained—if it would ever rain—sage smell would seep into the valley. There were signs for wineries, too, and a pile of twisted former cars and trucks, and a row of old Fords, salvaged but not yet renovated.

The old road wound through barren suede hills. We passed the homestead of a local white family who homeschooled five kids, all of them musical, Dave and Sue explained, playing banjo, mandolin, fiddle. The place felt bucolic, unremarkable. To think of it as the site of a massacre seemed fantastical.

On a rainy night in May thirty years earlier, my first night ever on the dry east side of the Cascades, I slept in an empty apple pickers' camp—springtime, not the season for picking—directly across the river from Chelan Falls. I was young and had taken a ranger job sight-unseen. I did not realize until the last minute you had to take a ferry to get there. Friends of mine, a couple, agreed to drop me off, and they brought their toddler, but we couldn't find a campground, so we set up our too-crowded tent not far from the Columbia River, storm-churned, lapping on small stones. It rained hard through the night. I don't remember seeing farm workers in the morning in the orchards nearby—standing on ladders to prune or driving tractors, spraying herbicide with raincoats on, hoods up—though surely they were there. I boarded the ferry, sleep-deprived and soaked, impossibly ignorant and hopeful.

Over the years, on many summer nights, I camped in the

same place, the former pickers' camp. The orchard had been torn out by then, replaced by Beebe Bridge Park, built as part of required mitigation for damage caused by dams downstream, with soccer fields, tennis courts, a picnic pavilion, and a campground. I'd pay twenty-five dollars to sleep on the lawn or in the back of the car, watch afternoon sun blast newly planted maples, and use the pay phone with a calling card number. I'd wake to find no-see-um welts on my forehead, boil water for instant coffee, and arrive in town to await the ferry with hair uncombed, sleeping bag still wet with dew. I knew nothing back then of the Chinese merchant who once owned a store at the exact same spot.

The Chinese store. On every map I could dig up, that's what it was called: the Chinese store. A merchant opened the store in 1860, and according to descriptions from the era, the building itself, a lean-to against a cliff with a roof made of logs covered with brush, wasn't too impressive, but the merchant sold everything: rice, flour, tools, ammunition, opium pipes. Opium, surely. He owned a forty-horse team and a rowboat with oarlocks for ten men. He grew gardens with green leafy vegetables and was, apparently, well-liked and respected.

"A stranger never appeared at the door of this old Chinese merchant," reads an 1892 article from the Spokane *Spokesman*, one with which I'd become intimately familiar, "who was not made welcome."

Turns out, the merchant opened his store at the perfect time—forty-niners were rushing from California toward rumored gold strikes in British Columbia—and it was about to get more perfect. In 1862, a Native man gave a white miner a canoe ride across the Columbia a few miles upstream from the store. The Native man pointed down through shallow green water to a sandbar below. Gold, he said. Right there. (Why tell?

Why right then?) The white man believed him, made a claim, and a clean quick $30,000. He got rich, and the sandbar was promptly named Rich Bar.

After that, the miners decided to stay. White miners took the easy gold, panned the surface, collected the nuggets, and left. Chinese miners moved in afterwards. They took over claims, dug more and dug deeper. They used wooden sluicing contraptions called "rockers" to skim gold from gravel by washing it through quicksilver (mercury) and rocking it back and forth, and they found what the white miners had missed. Of course, this created tension.

"There was not an inch of the river left untouched by the Chinese," reads one white old-timer's account of the era. "They snuck millions of dollars in gold dust like flour through Portland back to China." White people weren't the only ones perturbed. "The Indians called them 'pigtail braids,'" the old-timer claims, "and resented their aloofness."

Not all of them, though. Wapato John, N'k'whilekin, of the Entiats, had a small trading post on the Columbia a few miles downstream from the Chinese merchant, where he traded furs to Hudson Bay Company men. Each winter, the Chinese merchant hired Wapato John to take his forty-horse pack string two hundred miles overland to resupply his store. For at least a decade, they worked together. Indigenous people were farming and avoiding the army, Chinese gold miners were sluicing river gravel and avoiding the government men who were demanding steeper and steeper taxes, and all the while, white explorers were treading through the mountains, in search of railroad routes. The whole region was in flux, crazy on edge.

Then comes the massacre.

From various sources, I cobbled together a murky outline. In 1875, somewhere near the Chinese store, a group of Chinese miners—maybe as many as three hundred—were pushed off a cliff into the river and died. Or maybe it wasn't three hundred people, maybe it was a three-hundred-foot cliff; some historians think the numbers get conflated. And maybe they were murdered first, and then pushed over the edge.

The most popular version of the story claimed the attackers came from the Methow, a drainage to the east of Chelan Falls, though they may have been Chelan or Wenatchi or Entiat people. All of them were, for a time, under the charge of Chief Moses, Quetalican, chief of the Sinkiuse-Columbia people—"a greater diplomat than a warrior," according to one biographer. When Chief Joséph of the Nez Perce famously fought the US Army until he could fight-no-more-forever, he tried to persuade Moses to join him, but Moses refused. Chief Moses stayed put and tried to keep the peace. To no avail. Fur traders had encroached, then miners, then explorers in search of a railroad route, and for centuries before them, reports of ruin had circulated. Three hundred years of colonizers. Three hundred years of disease. Native people knew entire nations in the east and on the plains had been displaced. Some like Joséph tried to fight. Some like Moses tried to negotiate. Nothing worked.

It makes sense that, in the face of all this, a handful of angry men might take their frustration out on the Chinese as the latest encroachers, or the least powerful ones. If they did, they would've acted from a kind of self-defense that's hard to condemn, and sympathy for their motivation made thinking about this event—and everything happening in America—feel more tenuous and urgent.

All through the winter, I studied the ridges on either side of the Columbia River. I noticed one high treeless bluff wide enough to hold a large group of people, maybe three hundred feet high, a couple miles upstream, but it didn't drop cliff-like to the river. A gentle slope at the bottom eased riverward, and that's the river after the dam; before the dam, the water would've been even further away. Victims could've died from the drop, but the bodies wouldn't land in the river. Downstream there were fewer spots. I'd even taken a long meandering hike through the hills past "No Trespassing" signs and through barbed wire looking for any cliff that dropped three hundred feet into the Columbia. No luck.

I hoped Dave and Sue would know more, and they did. Sue pointed to one steep sloughed bluff near the Walmart on the far side of the river. That was a place, she said, where Chinese people who farmed land in the countryside and drove their goods into town to sell used to park their wagons. An old-timer told her how he and some buddies locked Chinese men in their wagons with the asparagus and onions and rolled them into the gorge for fun.

Who knows if the gruesome tale were true? It'd been told, it seemed, with nonchalance, the way boys will brag about torturing animals, daring you to condemn them. The time frame was suspicious, too, since most Chinese people were long gone by the turn of the century, unless the storyteller was very *very* old. For her part, Sue wasn't offering any commentary. Dave entertained us, instead, with stories of his days as a firefighter, how all the time they'd get called to respond to accidents on this road, a perfect getaway for underage partiers, scenic and safely out of town.

Finally, we stopped at a wide spot in the road, a gravel pullout, and walked a few steps out onto an exposed rock ledge—no guardrails, no warning signs—from which you could peer down into the gorge where a stream of brilliant green water meandered among rocks iron-tinged like the redrock canyons of Southern Utah. What water we could see had been released through the dam. Since the 1920s, much of what pours from the mouth of Lake Chelan gets diverted through a tunnel to the powerhouse, though sometimes, in early summer, the amount released, the so-called spill, will swell to a torrent. Each year a few kayakers get permission to run the Class V stretch described as "several drops from five to twenty feet high, numerous cascades, bedrock chutes, and large, deep pools."

We couldn't see any of that grandeur from the overlook. We couldn't see town either, couldn't see orchards, couldn't see the Columbia even. Every place within view was a barren bluff or a near-cliff. A few live pines and black snags clung to rock protrusions. A breeze picked up and cirrus clouds soft-streaked the blue sky. We inched cautiously toward the edge. It was so steep we left Daisy in the car. A few rocks skittered loose and fell. Sue pointed out some caves that may have been mining shafts, hand-dug in the hope of finding hard rock veins. Who knows how the miners accessed those either? Ladders, likely, or nimble feet.

Suddenly, Dave stepped back and grew somber, a radical shift, as Dave's not a somber guy. He began to tell another story, haltingly. One August day years earlier, a buddy had been out here with some friends, and somehow took a wrong step.

Dave stopped, then continued.

The guy fell to his death from this exact spot.

I stood in silence. What was there to say? It's hard to hear something this intimate from someone you don't know well, harder yet to stand in the exact place where tragedy occurred. It was easy to imagine what happened, easy to imagine it happening again. The rock on which we stood jutted out so far it seemed nearly cantilevered, a flat rock no bigger than legroom in an airplane seat, and a very long drop.

The wind blew. Sadness lingered. We got back in the car.

In *Oh What a Slaughter: Massacres in the American West 1846-1890* Larry McMurtry uses the Oxford English Dictionary definition of *massacre*, which includes words like *shambles, butchery, general slaughter, carnage* to compare the aftermath of such an event to a meat shop. It's not the number of murdered that qualifies an event as a massacre, but the ferocity, the crazy volition, the intent to harm and the tendency to escape attention, justice, and, for a while, history. In the end, McMurtry argues, blood wins out, and stories surface.

But here's the thing: other massacres had survivors. Park rangers at Whitman Mission National Historic Site outside of Walla Walla can recreate the 1847 massacre of Marcus and Narcissa Whitman in excruciating detail because two dozen children survived, were taken hostage, and lived to tell the tale. We know for certain, for example, that Narcissa was shot, while Marcus took a hatchet in the back of the head.

Sue Clouse knew a man who told a story set shortly after Rocky Reach Dam began to raise the Columbia River level in the 1960s. The man's brother and some buddies went down to Beebe Bridge—right where the Chinese store had been—to watch the water rise and saw several bodies float to the surface. An archaeologist later confirmed for me the feasibility of this occurring depending on the speed of the impoundment, the associated local currents, and how those currents undercut riverbanks where bodies—skeletons at least—may have been preserved. They raked them to shore to collect what Chinese jewelry and coins they could, then let them float downstream. On a nearby bluff, on another day, the same man told Sue, his brother found a skull with a hatchet in it.

But how could we know if that was true?

Back when the merchant ran the Chinese store, rumors would have circulated about a group of Chinese merchants who'd been rounded up and murdered by Northern Paiute down in Baker City, Oregon—some three hundred miles southeast—their bodies strewn on the road in pieces. Some said the bodies had been buried, then dug up, scoured clean, packed in wagons, and shipped home to China. He surely heard the rumor and others like it.

But how could he know if they were true?

*

From the overlook, Dave, Sue, and I rode in silence as the road descended around steep switchbacks over washboard gravel to meet asphalt in the tiny town of Chelan Falls. We passed orchards—apples, still, not so many grapes—with pickups parked between the rows, abandoned warehouses and a large riverside park with wide lawns and picnic shelters where Mexican families gather on Sundays in summer, then further downstream, huge new waterfront homes, the kind designed, it seems, to hold houseguests by the horde on weekends, with impeccable landscaping watered by sprinklers on timers. The place seemed a mix of rich and poor, old and new, in the middle of nowhere, on the way to nowhere, so much so that it was hard to remember how once this was a major thoroughfare, the way everyone would come.

Downriver a few hundred miles, a vibrant cosmopolitan culture flourished along the Columbia River throughout the 1800s. Native people gathered at Celilo Falls for centuries. After Lewis and Clark traveled through in the early 1800s and Hudson's Bay Company set up Fort Vancouver near present-day Portland in 1852, Russians, Scotsmen, and Polynesians, trappers and soldiers and cattlemen congregated, too. They traded furs and weapons, tools and jewelry; they transported crops and spoke Chinook, the pidgin trade language.

But if there ever was an idyllic era of multicultural inclusion, it didn't last long. By the end of the century, most Chelan people had been herded onto the Colville Reservation; Chinese people, excluded by law and intimidated everywhere, disappeared from the region almost entirely. White settlers planted apples. In the 1930s, dust bowl migrants came to pick them, and when those men left to fight World War II, the US government started recruiting workers from Mexico, as part of the Bracero program. Many of them stayed.

*

Over the winter, after a flurry of news stories about ICE raids near the orange groves where I grew up in California, I began to wonder if the persecution was affecting people closer to home. I called Vanessa Gutierrez, a lawyer with Northwest Immigrant Rights Project, to ask. Things were bad, she told me, as bad as she's ever seen. Both documented and undocumented workers were being deported every day. If someone had a misdemeanor offense on their record, possession maybe, or a failure to pay child support, they would be deported, absolutely. No questions asked. That used to be rare. Now, there was a denaturalization task force looking for excuses to deport. Even professionals who had been in the region for decades were being targeted. Every day something new. Stress levels skyrocketing.

Everything felt in flux, crazy on edge.

At last, we crossed the Columbia and arrived at Beebe Bridge Park where the Chinese store once stood. We'd been here before, of course. Sue once owned a roadside coffee shop not far down the road and passed this way daily. I'd slept here countless nights. But this time, as we walked from the side of the highway, we saw the place anew through the lens of history. We speculated about slopes into which lean-tos could've been built, and noted the flatter ground, too, perfect for gardens, and a sandy beach protected from the wind, an easy spot to land a boat of supplies. I'd convinced myself, naively, that we'd discover some hard evidence, an artifact or a scar. When I worked on trails, we'd find relics of settlers or miners in the woods all the time: axe heads and mattocks, bullet casings, boot heels, sometimes a rotted log sill where a cabin once stood. At Beebe Bridge, there was nothing.

Since Rocky Reach Dam had raised the water level, I decided to check out the shallow river bottom on the leeward side of a bedrock outcrop. Dave and Sue sat on the beach in the warm sand with Daisy while I waded barefoot, my toes sinking into muck, frigid spring runoff soaking my rolled-up jeans, and predictably found nothing.

Did they learn about the Chinese miners in school? I asked. Never.

The Chinese immigrants mined and farmed, and later built the railroad; they set up businesses and over time faced every variety of discrimination from taxes to exclusion to violence. In 1864 Washington Territory passed a law titled "An Act to Protect Free White Labor Against Competition with Chinese Coolie Labor and to Discourage the Immigration of the Chinese in the Territory." In 1871, an angry mob of whites and mestizos in Los Angeles shot, hanged, and mutilated the bodies of eighteen to twenty Chinese immigrants. In 1882, the federal Chinese Exclusion Act was signed into law, preventing all Chinese workers—"skilled and unskilled laborers"—from entering the country, and marking the first time the United States restricted immigration based on race and class. In 1885, in Rock Springs, Wyoming, twenty-eight Chinese coal miners were killed by a white mob, setting off a spate of violence throughout the region. A few short months later, seven hundred Chinese residents of Tacoma were forcibly expelled.

No wonder the history wasn't taught in school.

I waded toward the water-sculpted rocks and pulled myself out of the water to warm my feet and admire the view. Basalt outcroppings, near black, punctuated the dry grass gold. Orchards grew on sloped ground, to allow cold air to drain—varied terrain yet another reason fruit grows so well in the region—and workers moved ladders as they pruned.

Finally, I returned to shore, and the three of us began scanning the ridges again for a massacre site, our ostensible reason for being here. We ran through the possibilities. Nothing made sense upstream. None of the downstream possibilities was within a mile.

Except one.

We could see the lookout clearly, the cantilevered rock on which we'd stood a couple of hours earlier, the ledge from which Dave's friend fell. The distance from the confluence, about a mile, was exactly right. So was the height, as Dave knows from the incident report after his friend's death: three hundred feet. If that was the site, it would mean the bodies fell into the Chelan River, not the Columbia, but none of the accounts had precisely specified.

The theory felt right, impossible to prove, easy to imagine.

So they approach: the attackers step carefully among the balsamroot, daisy-yellow flowers, knowing that when the flowers die, they'll crumple loudly, a sound too much like a rattlesnake's rattle. This time of year, while flowers still bloom, a snake is a snake. The attackers gaze down at the Chinese store and gardens, the forty-horse team, the ten-person boat docking with supplies. They murder the miners—five of them or fifteen, thirty or three hundred—and push them over the edge.

Chapter Two
WALLA WALLA

Revisit the map of Washington State and you find Walla Walla tucked in the bottom right-hand corner. The once bustling center of commerce is now a modest-sized town surrounded by rolling wheat fields, hemmed by the flat-topped Blue Mountains, home to three colleges, a maximum security state prison, and dozens of wineries. When, in fall 2017, I took the short-term job teaching at Whitman College in Walla Walla after thirty years in the woods, I landed in town—Country Mouse turned City Mouse—out of place, but full of wonder, wowed by streetlights, garbage pickup, patisseries that stayed open late. Even the silly-sounding name delighted me. Walla Walla, from the Cayuse meaning "many waters," is a dry place by Pacific Northwest standards, having many small creeks, but no big river.

Late August temperatures hovered in the high nineties, too high even for the east side of the Cascades, and smoke choked the sky. Wildfires burned everywhere in the region and seemingly everywhere in the whole dry tinder universe, and yet, in Walla Walla, everywhere you turned you'd find tidy houses with well-tended lawns. I was obsessed with the lawns: the green green grass and the sidewalks swept of leaves and the neighbors on the weekends in work gloves and shorts, foreheads sweating, weeding beneath the shrubs, tending roses, roses blooming still. Such motivation! What I once would have disparaged as blind conformity now seemed more worthy, if not exactly a political act, at least a community-minded gesture. In a world where so much felt out of control, here as antidote, a simple impulse: people taking care of what they could. Meanwhile, on campus, with access to boundless resources, I parked myself—a kid in a candy shop—day after day in front of one of two microfilm machines at the library and slipped back 150 years.

From *Wapato Heritage*, I had chased a footnote to an entry in the 1906 *History of North Central Washington*, a heavy hardcover tome that arrived in Stehekin by mail from the regional library, compiled by one Richard Steele. These colorful county-by-county histories, I'd later learn, were popular at the turn of the last century and sometimes took liberties with facts. This one, the so-called Steele history, was no exception. It confirmed the basic outline of the massacre: the proximity to Chelan Falls, the three-hundred-foot cliff, the Indigenous attackers. In Walla Walla, I unearthed a dozen more massacre mentions, and each time I did, the same details would reappear, often in the exact same phrasing. Where did these details come from? All evidence pointed to a single newspaper article from 1892 from the Spokane *Spokesman*. Oft-quoted. Hard as hell to find.

One weekend, I traveled to a regional history conference, trying to find someone, anyone, who knew more about these miners, and ran into my friend Larry Cebula, a historian who's studied the people of the Columbia Plateau for years. Did he know anything about the massacre? He didn't. We sipped sweet cocktails at a hip new basement bar in Spokane. Larry was skeptical.

"The only primary source is a newspaper article written seventeen years after the supposed event?"

I nodded. I got where he was heading. "But why would anyone make up a story like this?"

"People love their massacres," Larry said with a shrug.

I had no idea what he meant and wouldn't have a chance to ask for many months.

The next weekend I stopped by Whitman Mission National Historic Site outside town. The hillsides rolled golden, shorn of crops, a patchwork with green grass, winter wheat newly planted. The site occupies a wide oxbow in the Walla Walla River—a small river, not wider than a creek—and cottonwoods by the water's edge shimmered yellow against blue sky. Roger Amerman, the park ranger on duty in the visitor center, told me the original name for the place.

"Pasxapa," he said. "The place of the balsamroot sunflower."

I loved learning this. I'd visited several times since moving to Walla Walla, not only because this was a massacre site, and I'd been thinking about massacres, but because I liked the place, pastoral and hemmed by the mesa-like Blue Mountains lined atop, these days, with wind turbines, bright white and spinning, and I liked talking to Roger, an enrolled member of the Choctaw Nation of Oklahoma who lived on the Nez Perce Reservation of Idaho—his wife's community.

I gazed out the window. Not a flower in sight.

The yellow daisy-like flowers got plowed under at planting time, he explained, but you'd see bunches in the spring. Pasxapu, he said, is what the people of this place called themselves.

A few visitors wandered a lawn marked with squared off spaces, the former foundations for a barn, a mill, a blacksmith's shop, a modest home, all built by the Whitmans nearly two hundred years earlier, and razed, too, nearly that long ago.

The Whitman Massacre—any massacre—is hard history. The Whitmans, Marcus and Narcissa, a doctor and his wife, were Christian missionaries, earnest converts of the Second Great Awakening, and among the very first whites to arrive via wagon from the East, along what would become the Oregon Trail. They arrived in 1836, in the wake of the Hudson's Bay Company just as the fur traders were pulling up stakes, so it was not as though the Pasxapu—whom white people call the Cayuse—weren't used to dealing with settlers. In the version I learned in school, Marcus and Narcissa lived among the locals peaceably for a while until in 1847, they were murdered along with eleven others, including children. Eventually five Pasxapu/Cayuse men confessed to the killings.

The movie reenactment, which I watched every time I visited, in part because my friend Larry was featured, shows Marcus Whitman standing upright with muttonchops and a suit coat preaching to the Cayuse people, who are intrigued at first, as spiritual seekers. But once Whitman gets to the fire and brimstone, they're not so enthralled. They stop attending services. Troubles intensify with the crazy number of new wagon train people arriving. The immigrants bring measles, and it's hard not to notice that while the white patients Whitman treats tend to survive, the Cayuse and other Indigenous people who come to him for help keep dying. Was it bad magic? Poisoning? No one knew about immunity back then. The Cayuse people ask the Whitmans to leave—nicely, repeatedly—but the Whitmans stay. The movie, at this point, turns toward melodrama: there's screaming and dishes breaking, a shirtless dark-skinned man running with a hatchet, rifle shots, and eventually, five bodies swinging in the public square.

After the massacre, the course of history shifted fast on the Columbia Plateau. The US Army moved in, and the Oregon Territory was established in 1848.

"Was it genocide?" I asked Larry.

"Not exactly," he insisted.

The question of whether it was genocide is complicated because, to some, the word connotes eradication of a people. The word emerged in response to the Holocaust when, in 1944, Polish-Jewish lawyer Raphael Lemkin coined it to describe Nazi policies of systematic murder. Lemkin later argued that colonization is "intrinsically genocidal," and in recent years this argument has gained traction. Governor Gavin Newsom officially apologized for treatment of the California Indians in 2019 by using the word, *genocide*. And the official conditions of genocide describe treatment of Indigenous people in the American West quite precisely: killing members of a group, forcibly transferring their children to another group, and/or "deliberately inflicting conditions of life calculated to bring about its physical destruction in whole or in part." But the people of the Columbia Plateau—the Yakama Nation, the Confederated Tribes of the Umatilla Indian Reservation, the Confederated Tribes of the Colville Reservation—are still around; after surviving the massacres of the 1800s, and steady systemic oppression, their populations are growing, their power, especially in the environmental realm, is rapidly expanding. They did not vanish in some distant, tragic past.

When I was a schoolkid in the 1970s, the Whitman story introduced me to the word *massacre* and its meaning conflated with bare-chested warriors wearing face paint, wielding machetes. But the xenophobia was tinged with confusing nuances. Even in those early history lessons, there was a sense that the massacre of the Whitmans had been justified. We weren't supposed to blame the Whitmans exactly, not even as much as the current share-the-blame reenactment does, but we weren't letting them off the hook, either. We were taught to carry pious guilt for how their murders led to horrid mistreatment of Indigenous people, but underneath lay a shrug of inevitability—violence begets violence—and most confusingly, the outcome did not, in the least, diminish the accomplishments of the stalwart white emigrants.

At the Whitman Mission, I walked the path around the foundations and followed irrigation ditches to a holding pond where snapping turtles slept on the shore, one on top of another. I came upon a stretch of the Oregon Trail along which you could see faux wagon ruts. There was a covered wagon, too, along the ruts, and a plaque saying it was built in 1974, the year in school I had to keep a fictional journal of a traveler on the Oregon Trail.

I wrote in the lively voice of a woman I pictured in a yellow bonnet, looking very much like Karen Grassle, who played Caroline Ingalls on *Little House on the Prairie*. Wagon train people were heroes to me, larger than life: the ones who survived, who endured, who hoped for something better. Maybe in the opposite order.

As I stood in the autumn sun, another visitor, a woman alone, approached. I'd crouched down to examine a small bucket fastened to the rear running board. For water? For waste? I dipped in my pinky: grease, lubricant for the axles.

"It's interesting," she said, meaning the wagon, the ruts, the massacre history, presumably. "And these people were amazing. I don't think we could do the things they did."

I disagreed on many levels, but I held my tongue.

Back at the college library, the screech-and-stop scrolling of microfilm, hour after hour, felt as familiar to me from my school days as a pencil pocked with chew marks on wide-ruled paper. To the college students who staffed the desk, the microfilm rolls were a novelty, like an eight-track tape. They smiled with a hint of pity each afternoon when I arrived. Clearly, I had nothing better to do. After a few weeks, at last, I hit pay dirt.

A newspaper article from 1892 popped up, not in the Spokane *Spokesman*, but in the *Chelan Falls Leader* under a cascading series of headlines: "Early Days on the River / Chinese Gold Hunters / Redskins made them go." Most of the three-column article described the setting: homes dug partially into the bluff with cedar board walls and log-and-brush roofs, and a well-respected merchant with a busy store. It was a lively and thorough read with a cringe worthy subplot about a "moon-eyed young fellow" tending a garden and lusting after "a dusky Indian maiden." I rushed through most of it, waiting for the massacre.

There'd been skirmishes up the Methow Valley to the east, the unnamed author claims, and then,

> When the Indians reached a point on the Columbia, a few miles below where Chelan Falls is now located, they discovered a number of Chinamen working on a bluff 300 feet above the river. The savages advanced cautiously and surrounded the celestials on three sides, leaving only the steep bluffs unguarded. Then began an uneven fight. The Chinamen were unprotected and unable to escape and they proved easy prey to their savage antagonists. How many were massacred was never known, but it is positive not one is left to tell the tale. It was an awful fight that sent terror into the hearts of other Chinamen along the river.

Larry's skepticism gnawed at me. Even if you found the article, he'd argued, you couldn't trust much unless it quoted eyewitnesses. This one didn't. It also lacked basic information. When exactly did the massacre happen? What day or month or season? What about the weather or the wind? What happened afterwards? Were the bodies mourned and buried? The attackers pursued? The crime prosecuted? And what about the location? The article placed the event not "a mile" from Chelan Falls, as I'd read elsewhere, but "a few miles below," which made the theory Dave and Sue and I concocted seem a whole lot less viable. The wobbly facts annoyed me, yes, but the racism rankled more—the "savage antagonists," the "hapless" Chinese, "easy prey" with "terror in their hearts."

In the late 1800s, the familiar caricature of the coolie appeared regularly in newspaper editorials all over the American West. With a bucktoothed grin and a long braid, the coolie loved to work for pennies and smoke dope underground, and as such, managed to come across as stupid and sinister at once. This newspaper description fell in the same vein. I reread the article hoping for some deeper sense of the Chinese merchant, some actual humanity. Like a Polaroid picture, the portrait remained underdeveloped: milky, hazy, barely translucent.

Chapter Three
WONG SAM

The *Wong Sam English-Chinese Phrasebook*, published in 1875 and distributed at Wells Fargo bank offices throughout the West, exposes a life riddled with anxiety. A pocket-sized volume, it had common phrases in English on one side of the column and Chinese figures on the other. A user of the phrasebook had to be able to read Chinese and at least some English. Or find a friend who could. The book wasn't for use like a tourist phrasebook you pull out at the hotel registration or the back of the taxi. The phrases were intended to be memorized, which means they were limited to ones you'd need often.

He assaulted me without provocation
I struck him accidentally
The men are striking for wages
Will you sell on credit?
Don't fear. I am not cheating you
I cannot trust you

The phrasebook was rediscovered and redistributed in 1991 by authors Jeffery Paul Chan, Frank Chin, Lawson Fusao Inada, and Shawn Wong in *The Big Aiiieeeee!: An Anthology of Chinese American and Japanese American Literature*. I learned about it watching a poor-quality video recording of a conference presentation the authors gave and immediately found the full text online. I was horrified and humbled.

I didn't understand until I read these entries how hard life had been for the Chinese. I'd read enough histories of the West to find them lurking around the edges, bit parts in B-movies, afterthoughts. Now the misperceptions rankled: That Chinese people came to America only long enough to make money and then hightailed it home. That they'd worked only on the railroad or in laundries. That they sold gold dust for cash and rushed their riches back to China. That they were sure, even, that their bones were sent back to China after death. They were part-timers, transients by choice. Foreigners when they came, foreigners when they disappeared. None of this was true, or it was half true, as it was of many of the Irish and Scottish and Norwegian, Swedish, and German immigrants who gave the arid West a desperate shot, then bailed out.

But here's the thing: the Chinese community was the largest single non-Native population in Eastern Oregon and Washington for nearly thirty years. In the late 1950s, John Esvelt, an amateur historian and Spokane engineer, wrote an oft-cited history, "Chinese Placer Mining on the Upper Columbia," in which he estimates the population along the Columbia River east of the Cascades in 1870 as "not more than 800 whites but 1500 Chinese." If that number is anywhere close to correct, and many later historians believe it is, the Chinese were the first non-Native settlers in the region.

But *settler* is the wrong word since every time they tried to settle, they were prodded along by laws or taxes or violence.

They were lying in ambush
He took it from me by violence
He cheated me out of my wages
He was choked to death with a lasso, by a robber

Every time I paged through the Wong Sam phrasebook, I thought of an old friend who liked to call himself a coolie. He was a white man who'd grown up in the 1950s, and in his youth, between seasons as a high school baseball star, he'd worked picking fruit and as a laborer on the railroad where he learned the slur. Later he'd ship out as a merchant marine and travel the world. By the time I knew him, he was in his early fifties and still doing physical labor on backcountry trail crews where we regularly walked ten to twenty miles a day and carried sixty-pound packs.

"The hotter, the better," he'd say, as he worked swinging a machete for ten hours a day in hundred-degree heat. "Call me a coolie," he'd say, and I'd cringe.

My friend knew the word was an insult. He'd worked side by side with Asian laborers on merchant ships, and he co-opted the label in solidarity, he believed, affection even. Even though he wasn't technically wrong to use the word—"coolie" derives from Tamil *kuli* and refers generally to any hired hand or unskilled laborer—the caricature of a coolie as always working and happy to work was condescending at best, dehumanizing at worst. The Wong Sam phrasebook drove home for me how insidiously the cartoonish name obscured the brutality Chinese laborers faced, how name-affixing turns into name-calling, and pretty soon there are people working hard, incredibly hard, who cannot even hold on to basic barrel-bottom hope: that you'll be paid next week, not cheated or evicted, or god forbid, suffocated in your room or choked with a lasso.

Before Thanksgiving, the grass in Walla Walla went dormant, gray as the sky. Icy fog hung heavy. A friend knitted me a wool hat, and I needed it bad. The only thing worse than the weather was the news. A Muslim ban in the works. DACA rescinded. For the first time in my life, I considered not listening. It had always struck me as a cop-out to say such a thing, the worst kind of shirking, but I couldn't take it anymore, how the headlines harped on who belongs, who doesn't, who gets heard, who gets silenced: workers losing the right to class-action lawsuits, children disappearing from government homes. Had it always been this bad? Had it ever?

Work grew busy. Research time evaporated. I figured there was nothing more to do, anyway, unless I could find the other 1892 article, the one from the *Spokesman*. From what I could tell, no library collection or government archive in the nation had a copy. I'd just about given up hope when, shortly after Christmas break, I thought to contact the newspaper itself, in its current incarnation, the Spokane *Spokesman Review*. One phone call and voila! A part-time archivist printed it on photo-quality paper and sent me a copy for twenty-eight dollars. Just like that. When I unrolled it on my kitchen table, I was utterly deflated.

It was the same article I'd read in the *Chelan Falls Leader*. The exact same description of the massacre. I rechecked the dates. The *Leader* piece came two days later. It was a reprint. Word for word.

Only this version had an even more troubling title, "Heathen Pioneers," and a lengthy subtitle: "They Came in Droves to Work the Placer Diggings—Interesting Ruins of Their Abodes at the Foot of the Chelan River—A Garden and the Sad Romance of Its Pig-Tailed Owner Who Died of A Broken Chinese Heart." I read the article, scanning past the short description of the massacre itself to soak in the overall tone: wistful, haunted, decidedly past tense.

The author is clearly writing in situ, at the place on the edge of the river where the Chinese store once sat, but the author remains unnamed and without gender. Whoever it is, they've visited the site as nostalgic pilgrimage, it seems, and they find the abandoned village looking like "a chicken coop after a Kansas blow." They describe a low fence of broken cedar pickets, mustard plants with yellow flowers blowing in the breeze, old stables where oats have gone to seed, and cabin remnants "the abode of snakes and rodents."

Only one line strays from rueful reverie: "With civilization," the author insists, the cabins will be torn down "and real progress will begin," as though the forced retreat of the Chinese merchant—the hero of the story also remains unnamed—was fated, inevitable, all part of a grand design.

The prose thickens with sensuality and eases into speculation. The "resort" consisted of couches, our author says, where you—dear reader—can imagine the pungent odor from an opium pipe and hear the rattle of the dice and the "indistinguishable jargon over the game of bung loo" while outside, as would-be gamblers pass, the "moon-eyed gardener" sits under the stars and "dreams and dreams and sighs and sighs."

I read until my own imagination ushered me back in time.

Step inside the store. See sacks of flour, sugar, and coffee, wooden barrels and tea crates labeled with faded Chinese letters, wagon wheels, bridles and straps, long-barreled rifles, baskets woven from beargrass and cedar bark for collecting vegetables, and heavy blankets of mountain goat wool, dyed with alder and willow bark, blueberry juice and charcoal. Watch the merchant tip gold dust from a knife onto a scale. He's a small man, five foot tall, eighty pounds, if he's average-sized, wearing a silk jacket, a long black queue. Behind him, shelves display fine stone pipes, ceramic buttons, silk fabric, straw hats, glass bottles of various colors and shapes, and ceramic urns filled with dried herbs used as medicines. There's kerosene, copper teakettles, colorful beads, and a woodstove in the center, ornately decorated, where in winter, men gather to play whistles and hand drums, music steeped in the thunder of horse hooves, the trill of spring birdcalls, an unrelenting keening.

Step outside when rising sunlight skims river riffles and the wind is thankfully calm—the only blessed calm all day—and scan the village anew: lean-tos against the bluff walls, logs for roof beams, narrow pine purlins topped with thin limbs woven like wattles, and cedar walls, board-and-batten tight. Plus ladders and wheelbarrows—hand-built, shallow, off-square—and shovels, buckets, rope, axes, picks. Men lounge by the river on decked logs, driftwood firs washed ashore or thick pines felled in shady draws, with their whipsaws leaning beside them unused while they take a break. Tents propped with peeled poles line the shore, and yes, the gardens too, summer lush, with leafy greens and herbs.

On a morning like this, our author reports, the lovesick gardener was found dead, and when the village was destroyed in the wake of the massacre—"the awful fight that sent terror through the hearts of other Chinamen along the river"—no one dared touch his garden.

The spell breaks. The syrup's too thick, the melodrama too overwrought. The author tugs at the reader's heartstrings for a couple of columns as if to say: massacres happen, sure, but unrequited love sells newspapers. In the end, this article I'd chased for so long, the work of a gifted writer with a keen eye for detail and a clear interest in history, chastised me. What's the point? Why sieve through the past for shiny baubles to piece into a story?

> *I arise at sunrise*
> *It is very expensive to live here*
> *He was suffocated in his room*
> *He was strangled to death by a man*
> *My family is at home, sure*

On weekends, I drove home along the Columbia, past gas stations selling sweet onions in ten-pound sacks, past the confluence with the Snake River where Lewis and Clark once camped, and through the Tri-Cities where the Hanford Nuclear Site processed plutonium for the bomb dropped on Nagasaki, and northward past fields of wheat shipped, increasingly, to China, and massive blue-tarped hay bales sporting, still, giant signs for Trump. In a hyper-urbanized world, it's tempting to consider landscapes like this as places apart, devoid of history or relevance, when in fact they're drenched in both.

An hour into the drive, the river swooped west, and I turned onto a shortcut straight north through Moses Coulee. I'd never known about Moses Coulee before taking this job. With a major interstate to the south, and a cross-state highway to the north, I'd had no need to drive this backroads route. No need to learn the geologic term, either. Coulee: pronounced the same as *coolie*. Coulee: an ancient river channel. Moses Coulee: formed by the rapid warming that caused Lake Missoula—a half-state-sized lake, larger than Lake Erie—to melt at the end of the last ice age eighteen thousand years ago. Moses Coulee: named for Chief Moses, whose people grew gardens of squash and corn and potatoes in the poor soil, washed away in the ancient floods, built back over time, protected by basalt cliffs. Moses Coulee: where the Chinese merchant would've traveled regularly, from Chelan Falls to Walla Walla, to resupply his store.

His trip would take four days by foot with an empty pack string, sixteen fully loaded.

Mine took four hours by car, either way. I rarely passed another car. I watched late daylight hit black cliffs trimmed with yellow-green lichen, subtle and stunning. I passed sagebrush and cattle grazing on grass beside prickly pear cactus in tight spiny bunches. Snow began to skitter like sand on the windshield. When the road rose back up, swooping onto the Waterville Plateau, and rock outcroppings began to appear—glacial erratics jutting vertically, ridiculously, out of the fields where our grocer likes to pheasant hunt—I knew I was close. Finally, at the top of McNeil Canyon, I could see the North Cascades and began my descent to the river, to Beebe Bridge Park. I parked on the roadside to gaze up once more at the rock from which Dave's friend fell, and imagined one more entry in the phrasebook:

They fell from a very high place
Strike that.
They were pushed

Chapter Four
AH CHEE

The displays in the newly renovated space at the Chelan Museum celebrated Native people and settlers in equal measure. When I asked for information about the Chinese miners, the volunteer on duty dug in the files for a single manila folder holding a handful of newspaper clippings, most of which I'd seen before. A tourist from Seattle stopped by looking for evidence of her grandfather. She was thrilled to find his name on a list of steamboat captains. Another woman who helped me pinpoint the location of a Chinese laundry became distracted by a photo of the Methodist church in the 1940s, in which she could name several elders. She'd left town for a while, she said, and now she's back, and at the sight of the photo she gave a short gasp; how strange to discover these men she knew as a child preserved in a photo-slip binder. The sense of reconnection coursed so strong it seemed almost to embarrass her.

I wasn't looking for an ancestor, or not one by blood. I was looking for the elusive Chinese merchant, the man described in some accounts as "a community pillar," but there was no photo of him in his Sunday suit among his brethren or behind the wheel of a steamboat, and no descendants stopped in on a rainy afternoon to find reassuring evidence of him. The thing about being a pillar is, over time, someone has to keep you propped.

The merchant's store could be fixed on the ground easily. Later in the afternoon, I'd walk, again, across the rain-wet lawn at Beebe Bridge Park carrying an enlarged photocopy of the 1887 survey plat with the place marked clearly: township and range, lat and long. The merchant's boat launch would have been right where pleasure boats and Jet Skis launch now. The crude cedar dwellings would've sat where motor homes park, and gardens would've stretched between the soccer goalposts or under the tennis courts. There was a gambling house and an opium den, and stables built by digging a deep ditch and walling it up with rocks, so the roof was nearly even with the ground. The store was the first commercial operation in North Central Washington, by several accounts, with a larger stock of goods than any establishment in a three-county radius. The whole bustling enterprise was big enough to merit the label of "village." But the merchant himself, the man at the center of it all, remains a mystery.

Does he speak with a loud voice? Does he persuade with the silver tongue of a snake oil salesman? Opine with abandon? Or has he mastered the noncommittal nod, never disagreeable, always eager to accommodate, so long as it's in exchange for cash or gold dust. In the evenings, in the haze of opium smoke, does he take part, or withdraw to a private space, safely apart?

This much I had learned: In the 1870s, an old merchant, who was considered very wealthy, supplied goods to all the miners along the river and travelers, too. Steamships were still a decade or more away, as was the first wagon road from the river to the lake, from Chelan Falls to Chelan. But fur traders still plied their wares via canoe, and cattlemen with small herds sometimes swerved west from the famous Cariboo Trail that ran from Oregon to British Columbia, and for any of them, a village—even a Chinese village—would be a welcome sight. They passed through, and they were always welcomed. According to the *Spokesman* article, a traveler could expect near luxury. "If he was hungry he was fed, and it was not a makeshift meal that was served, either, but the best the larder afforded."

That's it. That's all I knew for sure.

Take a half-step from the tight tether of facts, and there was more to infer. The old merchant probably came from Guangdong, one of thousands who fled wars and famine in the nineteenth century in search of the elusive Gam Saan, the Gold Mountain. He'd travel by small boat, a junk, down the lush humid waterways of the Pearl River Delta to the city of Guangzhou, where a local commissioner had confiscated and burned three million pounds of opium in 1839 to start the first of two Opium Wars with England, and then by sea sixty-nine nautical miles to Hong Kong where at last he'd board a sailing ship bound for Gold Mountain. The trip from Hong Kong to San Francisco or Portland took six to eight weeks and cost thirty to fifty dollars, so most laborers either borrowed money or signed a contract to work off the cost when they arrived.

But this man wasn't a laborer; he was a merchant, a designation, in China, of class more than vocation, and while there's a slim chance he built his purchasing power in the gold fields of California, it makes more sense that he came with cash. Beholden to no one. On the prowl for opportunity.

Say he landed in Portland. From there, he'd take the usual route, east along the Columbia River then north, through Walla Walla. Three decades after the Whitman Massacre, the town was abuzz with commerce, a jumping-off place for miners, with a handful of Chinese-owned businesses. Maybe the merchant stopped in to check out the future competition and/or suppliers, and decided to keep moving. Outside of town, he'd find hillsides newly planted in winter wheat, and along the route, everywhere: horses, horses, horses. The Cayuse people had become expert horse handlers in the two centuries since the Spanish introduced the animals to the continent. If the merchant didn't know how to ride or wrangle before, he'd learn now.

Onward toward British Columbia. He'd pass through Moses Coulee between steep basalt cliffs, black and limned with lichen, the valley bottom covered in bunchgrass, with trees a rare sight, some cottonwood or willow in the draws. He'd burn cow patties for warmth, kill deer or bighorn sheep for food. He'd carry his possessions tied in two sacks on either end of a long pole over his shoulders. Nothing to differentiate him from any other Chinese man making the same trek. Nothing until he stood alone atop the Waterville Plateau and gazed down five hundred feet at the Columbia below, the Columbia again, but wilder and emptier than at Portland. He'd see cedar driftwood charge over rapids and circle in eddies: wood enough to burn, hell, wood enough to build with. He'd see the mouth of the Chelan River, and across from it, a wide flat space for gardens and a sandy beach from which to launch a ferry or barge.

For close to twenty years, that's where he'd stay.

The 1878 census of the Columbia River Region, available via Washington State archives online, handwritten in ledger-like columns in the clear looping script of the day, lists 130 Chinese persons. All men. All between ages fourteen and forty-three, most in their twenties. All born in China. All listed by the same profession: miner. Most, but not all, unmarried. Most vexingly, all have the same first name listed: "Ah." I looked it up. "Ah" isn't really a name; it's a non-name, a prefix, both affectionate and diminutive, something like "Uncle" or some say "Bachelor."

The oldest entry among them is "Ah Chee" thirty-eight years old.

Could this be the merchant by the river?

Both the Steele history and the original *Spokesman* article describe the Chinese merchant at Chelan Falls as "old." Would thirty-eight be old enough to be considered old? If you consider the fact that life expectancy hovered around forty, then, yes, for sure. I ran a search for "Ah Chee" elsewhere in the region and found one man with this name in Walla Walla in 1866 accused of running a gaming house, though a grand jury did not find evidence to indict. If this was, by chance, the same Ah Chee from the census, and if the same Ah Chee was in fact the merchant at the Chinese store near Chelan Falls, running a gaming house fits the entrepreneurial mold. The theory would require him, for a time, to be in two places at once: Chelan Falls and Walla Walla. That wouldn't be impossible, as I well knew.

In the fact-scarce space I'd landed myself in, this name seemed somewhere close to truth: closer than "hapless" or "prey" or even "coolie."

The merchant by the river, I decided—for the sake of the story, for the sake of humanizing this elusive community pillar—had a name: Ah Chee.

Chapter Five
EARTHQUAKE

On Saturday, December 14, 1872—a dozen years after Ah Chee opened his store and three before the massacre—a 7.4 earthquake shook the region so hard a chunk of mountainside broke off near Entiat, not far from Chelan Falls. The landslide blocked the Columbia River completely for hours.

Just past a lengthy section of Highway 97A lined with chain-link fence to keep bighorn sheep from wandering into SUVs, a large sign marks the spot. On a rainy spring day, I pulled over beneath a rocky cliff and beside the sign—small white letters routed into splintering wood, not much as heritage markers go—and gazed across the highway and past railroad tracks to where the Columbia ran wide and slow. How wide was it 150 years ago? A half mile? More? I stared up at the cliff face through which a ribbon of red runs—a hump-shaped vein of oxidized iron—and imagined the shuddering earth, the shattering noise, the animals braying, the river charging hard, storm-surge waves breaking, granite chunks clashing like outsized gladiators or rams in rut, the sloshing, the splashing, the shock.

Like an omen. Or maybe a culmination.

Ah Chee had surely heard dark rumors before the earth shook. Everything that happened on that stretch of river passed through his store. But if men claimed trouble loomed, hell, trouble always loomed. Part of a good merchant's job is to quell unrest, to provide whatever eases the burden of river life, to commiserate, if not quite agree, and always, always, to listen. Knowing as much about your clientele as possible—or not knowing—could make or break a business anywhere, but especially way out here. Men who frequented Ah Chee's store were bent and broken, broke and lonely, far from home. They smoked and drank and complained and lied. They also spent money, more and more every day. Twelve years now he'd had his store. Business had never been better.

But change was afoot. A short year earlier, Sam Miller, J. C. Wright, and the Free Brothers had taken over a ramshackle trading post near the confluence with the Wenatchee River. (The original owners had been arrested for selling liquor to Native people—one of the first laws established with the Oregon Territory in 1849—and were serving time in prison in Walla Walla.) Miller and his partners settled in and married Wenatchi women, a bold move that siphoned business from Ah Chee since, from the beginning, the Native people had been among his most loyal customers. Soon, the ambitious newcomers would drain almost all of his business away. Sam Miller would plant peach pits, according to lore, and thus begin Wenatchee's orchard tradition. For a time, he'd even name the town after himself: Millersburg. For now, Miller's Trading Post posed little threat. The place sat forty long miles downriver from Chelan Falls, for one thing. Two days travel heading up, a full day heading down. Plus, Ah Chee would know how to build the rockers and sluice boxes the placer miners preferred. He'd grow leafy greens white men never bothered to grow and medicinal herbs used by Chinese doctors and Native healers alike.

Still, change was everywhere. No denying it. By the 1870s, trappers had abandoned the region; no more market for furs. Cattle drives up the Cariboo Trail had slowed to a stop when thousands of meat-eating gold miners moved on from British

Columbia. A few miles from Ah Chee's store an old Black man named Antoine lived in a small cabin and kept watch for Sil-so-saskt, chief of the Entiats. Antoine had been born in Africa, shipped to America in chains, fought in the Civil War, and crossed the continent on foot.

Talk about change.

Farther along 97A, I stopped at the riverside park in Chelan Falls near the confluence of the Chelan River and the Columbia. From there, you have a full view of Beebe Bridge Park and of the bridge itself, the second one built on this site since 1919. Before then, crossing had been crazy. Settler diaries describe with abject admiration, near awe, women herding horses through the churn. For river-freight, Ah Chee would have to beach his famous ten-man row boat expertly in an eddy behind the sculpted rocks where I'd sat with Dave and Sue Clouse. For travel, he'd use a dugout canoe, carved from a single red cedar— borrowed or bought from Native people—far lighter, faster, and maneuverable than the rowboat. Not until the 1890s would steamships make it this far upriver. Even then, there'd be spectacular wrecks.

The original Beebe Bridge wasn't intended for human travel, but for water: the most crucial commodity in dry country. The 1919 suspension bridge, constructed at a cost of over $75,000, carried spring water in two wooden flumes to an orchard owned by the Beebe family. At the time, it was the largest privately owned bridge in the world, and by the late 1940s the Beebes boasted the largest family-owned apple orchard in a state known for apples. By the late 1950s—a short decade later—they'd sell out to the state to make way for hydropower. Construction of this newest bridge was completed in 1963 to accommodate the broader lazier river as water backed up behind Rocky Reach Dam, one of the largest and last of the fourteen dams on the Columbia to be built, one that produces gobs of clean cheap electricity, which has lately attracted hordes of data farms, large air-conditioned warehouses that sop up megawatts of public power to cool our collected photos and emojis stored in the so-called cloud.

Which is to say: the 1870s weren't the only era of astonishing change.

Of all the customers at Ah Chee's store, the Native people may have been most attuned to trouble, expectant, alert. They'd been listening to the prophet Smohalla, a Wanapum, and their own Wenatchi prophet, too, Patoi. They'd gather to dance and to listen to the prophets predict dark shadows on the moon and bigger changes too. The earth itself, the prophets told the dancers, would shake in fury to push encroaching white men back and to test the mettle of the Indigenous people.

As though they hadn't already been tested. Nearly decimated by smallpox brought in by white trappers at the beginning of the century, the people of the Columbia Plateau had bounced back. They'd become experts with horses. They'd adopted farming. Lt. Henry H. Pierce, who came to survey the region in 1882, admired large swaths of cultivated crops, and long before Sam Miller set up shop, Wapato John had luck growing potatoes, for which he was given the name Wapato, the Chinook word for potato. Wapato John also planted the first apple trees in the region—grown from seeds from England via Fort Vancouver—and ran more than one thousand head of cattle. He lived on the hillside above Entiat, where Old Antoine lived, and he ran his own small trading post, halfway between Ah Chee's and Sam Miller's.

But the white man's grip was cinching tighter. In 1855, Isaac Stevens, the first governor of Washington Territory, had convened a treaty council in Walla Walla. There representatives from the Chelan, Wenatchi, Entiat, and Yakama peoples ended up relinquishing a collective 10.8 million acres—more than ten million!—in an "exchange" into which many felt duped.

Native people were determined to retaliate. Whites wouldn't tolerate retaliation. The people of the Columbia Plateau were dispersed and outnumbered and tried various strategies. Some, like the Nez Perce, settled with limited sovereignty on reservations until white men found gold, and all bets were off. Chief Joséph famously led them in war and retreat in 1877. Others like the Yakama, led by Chief Moses's brother Kwilninuk, fought the Walla Walla treaty from the beginning, only to surrender in Chewelah to the east. Chief Moses, for his part, negotiated with the whites for nearly forty years, eventually losing nearly all the land he'd been promised. Once he asked a man to count all the grains of sand on a river bar.

"There are too many," the man said.

"It's the same with the white men," Moses said. "There are too many."

One story simmered under the surface for more than a hundred years: In the summer of 1858, over one thousand US Army troops, nearly twice the estimated population at the time, convened in the region supposedly to settle the unrest. The soldiers were "spoiling for a fight" when they heard rumor of a white man murdered in Moses Coulee. General Robert Garnett led 314 men with 224 pack animals north to flush out the "hostile Natives." They had a hard row of it, enduring "frequent bog hols and yaller jackets" as they followed the Wenatchee River north from its confluence with the Columbia. By the time they stumbled upon a group of 70 Wenatchi people collecting nuts and berries along the White River, the soldiers were antsy and pissed.

From there, the narrative turns brittle, easy to crack. In one version of the story—the kinder gentler version—the US Army captured fifty Wenatchi women and children, burned their lodges, and stole their cattle and horses. The soldiers found the supposed "hostiles," shot some and hanged others. In a darker version, soldiers murdered every man, woman, and child on sight—the number of victims is unknown, an entire village worth—except one boy who was tending horses in the hills. The boy escaped and lived to tell the tale of the so-called White River Massacre—yet another buried massacre, how many might there be?—only recently rediscovered by Methow Valley historian Richard Hart at the urging of the Wenatchi community.

In the midst of the bedlam, the unraveling, women rarely appear in written records except as victims. They slip into the shadows of history, their hands work worn, bodies stretched by childbirth, hardened by the weather, but buoyed by this place, the circle of life—sage grouse and squirrels in spring, the yellow arrowleaf balsamroot spreading light across the green hills, in summer the trips to the mountains, and the sheer exuberance of movement and plenty, berries and mountain goats, trade with people from over the hills, the Sauk, the Skagit, salmon in the fall, and bighorn, and winter again—grounded by their place in this place, the presence of ancestors and the stories that bind them here. So they're dancing and watching the heavens. If, on one hand, the prophets were wily opportunists who learned basic astrology by reading the farmer's almanac, like self-proclaimed prophets in any era, they also hit a powerful nerve by tapping into very real fear, well-simmered rage, and desperate uncertainty: how would these children live, where, what forces beyond their control could wreak such havoc, and why, and would greater powers ever reverse the horrors?

They would, Smohalla insisted. Very soon.

The possibility of something, anything, breaking open in the face of the infuriating escalation, the unending crescendo, had to feel warm in the gut as dancing all night by a bonfire under a half-obscured moon.

*

And so the quake hit.

The sound echoed in the river canyon loud as an avalanche, like the whole world bursting open. Backwater flooded gardens, soaked flour supplies and sugar, wrecked boats, and washed away lumber left too close to shore.

The rocks tumbled across the river and created a dam across which several young Chinese miners ran back and forth in glee or terror or both. At dawn the following day, Wenatchi women went to gather water and found the river entirely dry. Not a drop to be had. The river—the mighty Columbia, the largest river running into the Pacific in North America—remained completely blocked for over twenty-four hours. When the river broke back through the rubble dam, the intrepid rock-hopping miners were stuck on the far side, and the whole region had changed.

Chimneys cracked in Olympia two hundred miles away. Ground broke open in Seattle.

At Sam Miller's trading post, the roof crashed in and the building separated in half. "I would've given every gray hair on my head to be out of the country," Miller later told reporters.

Wapato John and his family had their sod roof collapse and cover them in dirt. They shivered in light snow through the night.

Old Antoine and everything he owned? Gone.

And directly across the river from Ah Chee's store, a fissure opened, forcing groundwater up. An intermittent geyser sprayed into the air twenty or thirty feet. For years Chinese miners had been digging diversion ditches, coaxing water toward the river to ease the labor of sluicing, to irrigate their gardens. Now this: a miracle.

Twenty miles past the earthquake site, I parked at a hairpin turn near a bluff along the highway—the regular road, not the stage-coach road—connecting Chelan to Chelan Falls. The water let loose by the 1872 earthquake sprayed right here, across from Ah Chee's store, for a year and then turned into a year-round spring, the same spring that would irrigate Beebe Orchards decades later.

Meanwhile, another spring erupted in the midst of the Native village along the shore of Lake Chelan, three miles northwest. But this one spewed sulfurous gas, so smelly you couldn't possibly live nearby. Families had to pack up and move in the icy dark of December. Compare that to the fresh water the Chinese had been gifted. Was this some kind of sick joke?

Brand-new interpretive signs from the Washington Department of Fish and Wildlife announced a new natural area at Beebe Springs. The signs described flora and fauna, geology, and acknowledged the Chelan and Wenatchi people, the fact of their existence if nothing of their particular perspective. On the day I visited, yellow-flowered antelope bitterbrush and snow buckwheat—with a tiny white flower, striped pink—bloomed, giving the rain-coppered hills a light brushed palette of yellow, pink, white, and green. On the horizon, pockets of dense white clouds settled in forested valleys, white as snow, frothy as foam. I hiked a narrow rocky trail to an overlook from which you can see shallow spawning channels carved by heavy equipment to better accommodate the salmon that have almost gone extinct, and native shrubs planted for the California quail that dash everywhere, their topknots wobbling comically. Earlier that morning, I'd watched a slow moving car pull out of a driveway, hit a quail, and leave it fluttering in half-life on the road shoulder.

On my bedside at home I'd been reading a book called *Timefulness* in which the author, Marcia Bjornerud, explains that geologic time moves slow, yes, but change happens fast. From my vantage point on the trail at Beebe Springs, overlooking a landscape bare enough to expose scars of erosion and glaciations, it was easy to see the earth as dynamic, ever in motion. Change is inevitable, but always a surprise. In the Pacific Northwest, we're smack in the Cascadia subduction zone. Beneath us slowly, constantly, the Juan de Fuca plate slips under the North American Plate. Pressure is building. Some geologists predict a quake 9.0 on the Richter scale could hit any time.

After the earthquake, the history books assert, some Native people showed up at Sam Miller's trading post crying for him to read to them from scripture. Others, who had resisted Jesuit missionaries for a half century, broke down and accepted Catholicism. Some accounts claim that immediately after the quake, Wapato John moved to town and became a devout Christian, but that's not entirely true. He would convert, and he would eventually move into Chelan, but for most of the 1870s and 1880s, he remained on the river. As did Ah Chee. For a while at least.

Within months, Ah Chee would begin to hear stories about Chinese miners being harassed up the Methow, the nearest drainage to the east. Maybe he shrugged it off. For the Chinese, trouble wasn't anything new. One oft-repeated story—one I'd discovered in a newspaper article in the manila folder at the Chelan Historical Society and later found repeated in histories of Chinese in the Pacific Northwest—was told to a historian by a white man named Emery Bayley, who claimed it was told to him by an acquaintance, who claimed it was told to him by his "pappa's pappa's pappa." Around 1863, Bayley reports, a small group of Indigenous people spied two Chinese placer miners working on a river bar. They had never seen a Chinese person before— "had never heard of such a being." They captured the two miners and called a meeting to decide what to do with the strangers. The odd-looking men clearly weren't white and certainly weren't Native, so it was decided: they must be devils! They executed the first two Chinese they ever saw.

An equally disturbing story is recounted by cattleman A. J. Splawn in *Ka-Mi-Akin: Last Hero of the Yakimas*. One day in

1864 while traveling near Wenatchee, he befriended two Chinese men who agreed to help him move his cattle upriver. The threesome ran into two Native men, one of whom immediately began whipping one of the Chinese with the handle of his riding whip. Splawn pointed a gun and ordered him to stop the beating. Which he did. The second Native man, according to Splawn, turned out to be Chief Moses. When Splawn returned the badly beaten man to his village, "a howl went up like the noise of a flock of wild geese fired into suddenly."

The worst incident, at least until the Chelan Falls massacre, occurred in May 1866 when Northern Paiute Chief Egan led an attack against a group of Chinese people trekking along Battle Creek in Idaho. Hundreds of warriors, both Paiute and Bannocks, surrounded the travelers and demanded they give up their guns, and when they did, turned their weapons on them. As many as fifty to sixty Chinese people died.

There had always been trouble, and there had always been reasons for trouble. The Chinese men came without women, who weren't allowed to emigrate. The men were young and lonely, and if that didn't cause trouble, what would? There was jealousy, too, over money. A successful businessman like Ah Chee would be a target even before freshwater started spewing out of the ground, ripe for dispute.

But if he was so used to it, how did he decide when to leave?

A few weeks earlier, I'd stopped at the Wenatchee Valley Museum and Cultural Center where copies of the handwritten ledgers from Sam Miller's trading post are archived. I took time from my own hardware store visit (sprinkler parts, zip ties) and grocery shopping (tortillas, yogurt) to sit alone in a sun-brightened room reading lists of people's hardware store and grocery purchases from 150 years ago. Records begin around 1868, and in the early years names listed look like white men, Native people, a few Chinese people. Ah Chee himself appears, in October 1872, buying boots and nails. Are these items he can't get himself? A trip to town for a few sundries? Impulse buys? After the earthquake, Ah Chee drops off the ledgers at Miller's store for two years. Maybe he was doing fine in his own business. Maybe his trips to Walla Walla took care of his needs. Hell, maybe he traveled to China, saw his family, took a look around, and hopped a ship back. Wherever he went, by 1874, he's back and shopping more frequently at Miller's. Ah Chee and dozens of Chinese men. In fact, by 1874, nearly all of Miller's customers have Chinese names: John China, Ah Wau, Ah Lping, Ah Chung, Ah Jim, Ah John, Ah June, Ah Chon, Ah Choy, Ah Fang, Ah Chang. Ah Chee is a big spender. His largest order is typical.

> *tobacco 1.00*
> *matches .50*
> *2 b. lead .50*
> *1 tea 1.00*
> *4 lb beans 1.00*
> *8 sacks flour 24.00*

After 1875, the year of the massacre, the ledger shows only white names for two years. Then Chinese names begin to reappear. But not Ah Chee's.

I left Beebe Springs, crossed the river, and took a hard left just before reaching the place where the Chinese store once stood. Another week of classes in Walla Walla called. The road climbed steep past fruit warehouses and new houses exposed on the spare hillsides. Ravines cut hard into the slopes. There used to be more trailers tucked into draws out here, hidden places with old machinery in the yard, empty oil barrels, broken-down cars, always cars, a few ponderosas to mask the place, a fence for dogs.

The new construction lacked landscaping, making the difference stark, and begged the eternal question in the West these days: how will they fare in a fire?

At the top of McNeil Canyon, where the land turns flat, I switched to a podcast to take me the rest of the long flat miles south. The topographic drama was all behind me, the mountains, the river, the gorge. Once you leave the coulee and cross the interstate, there's only farmland, industrial and flat. What little relief there is, geologically and visually, remains obscured, almost always, by haze: wildfire smoke or winter fog or smog. That's why so few of my friends could figure out how I'd grown to love this landscape and to love the little town in the wheat fields where I was headed. But I did love it, and I knew it had to be my own affection that made me keep imagining that when Ah Chee felt the need to leave, Walla Walla is where he went.

He'd been traveling to Walla Walla regularly for supplies for years. He had to notice the changes over time. By 1872, Walla Walla was bigger and busier, and far more Chinese, than the town he left to make his fortune on the river. Soon the census would count more than five thousand residents in Walla Walla, more than six hundred of them Chinese. They did every job imaginable, every job available. If you count all the territories in the West, they were working in all sixty-three industries listed by the Trades Assembly. The railroad brought more jobs yet. One common misconception is that Chinese people came to work the railroad, and then stayed, when often it was the other way around. The rail line between Walla Walla and Wallula began construction in 1871 and lasted until 1875. Main Street boasted nine laundries in no time. If Ah Chee had run a gambling house in the 1860s, it had been replaced by at least a half dozen new ones.

Maybe the winter after the earthquake Ah Chee decided to visit Walla Walla for the New Year's celebration on the first full moon of February. Firecrackers in the snow. Young men in too-big boots. Maybe it felt like a homecoming. Or maybe he felt like a stranger. Maybe he thought: it's plain too many people. He was no longer a city guy if he'd ever been one. His horse skills, his boat skills, even his rapport with the Native people: none of it would count for much in a burgeoning mini-metropolis. Plus the trouble brewing wasn't only on the river and wasn't only with the local inhabitants. There were clashes among the Chinese population, stemming from family clan loyalty or competition between the six powerful companies for whom most Chinese laborers worked.

Then there were the whites.

Since Ah Chee was of the merchant class, he'd likely learned to read English back home in Guangdong. He could read the newspapers. In years past, economic relations between China and the US had looked positive. The US State Department under William H. Seward had granted China most favored nation status as a trading partner in the Burlingame-Seward Treaty of 1868. The future for immigrants like him had seemed bright, but tensions in the West were undermining diplomatic ambitions in the other Washington. Meanwhile, news from China announced the end of civil war; the last of the Taiping army was defeated in 1871. Ah Chee could catch a ship and sail to Guangdong, return home a success. Instead he returned to his store. Why?

Census records offer one possibility. The 1878 census lists 29 of the 130 Chinese miners along the Columbia River as married. Whether this meant they were married to someone in China or to someone in North America is unclear, but Ah Chee was one of them. Maybe he was married and didn't want to leave his wife.

Whatever the reason, after the earthquake he returned to his store until at some point, he—or they?—suddenly pulled up stakes and left.

Chapter Six
CHEE SAW

It shouldn't be hard to find the border of the United States of America, but outside of Chesaw, Washington, miles from any major highway, I wasn't finding it easy. In the age of build-the-wall paranoia and GPS precision, the international dividing line between the US and Canada at the forty-ninth parallel showed nowhere. Not on the ground. Not on a screen. Google sent me insistently to drive-across ports miles away, to the west and the east, at Oroville and Midway. My map showed only this: the border lies exactly 3.2 miles north of Chesaw.

Chesaw is the only town in the United States named for a Chinese person—the only one!—but it's a long way from where most Chinese people lived. Most nineteenth-century Chinese immigrants settled in Olympia, Seattle, Tacoma, and Bellingham, the string of forest-fringed cities along the Salish Sea. Chesaw, in the Okanogan Highlands—a broad unpopulated swath of rangeland and wetlands, orchards and farms, low mountains pocketed with pines—is three hundred miles northeast of Seattle, a four-hour drive northeast of Chelan, and a long way from anywhere.

I made the trek because I had a hunch.

Chee Saw, the man for whom the town is named, arrived in 1878 at the start of the mining boom and built a one-room log cabin along Myers Creek on land owned by his Okanagan wife, Susan

Lum. The mixed-raced marriage wasn't unusual. There were far more Native women than men in the territory due to illness and wars—as many as six to one—and far more Chinese men than Chinese women since the Chinese government did not allow women to emigrate, a scheme perhaps to bring the men home after their sojourns, richer, ready to settle down.

For Chee Saw, there was at least one more good reason to marry. Chinese men weren't allowed to own land in Washington Territory in 1878, but since much of the land in the upper Okanogan Valley had recently been deeded to the Confederated Tribes of the Colville Reservation (twelve total including the Entiat, Chelan, Wenatchi, Methow, Okanagan, Sinkiuse-Columbia, and Nez Perce) via treaty, Susan Lum could.

So Chee Saw and Susan settled in this open country—ripe for mining and farming and cattle ranching, or all of the above. They ran a small store, and, over time, raised six children: Agatha, Julia, Theresa, Christine, Maggie, and Joe. Sometimes histories call Julia his wife. Sometimes they call Chee Saw, Charlie Chesaw. Sometimes they call him Joe Chee Saw, but Joe is their son, a well-known rabble rouser, who will die young and be buried in Osoyoos, just across the border in Canada.

Usually Chee Saw is just Chee Saw. He was tall for a Chinese man, they say, and better looking than most. He greeted visitors amiably at the local hotel. He grew vegetables and sold them for miles around. He'd famously walk to Republic, forty miles over the mountains to the east, with two sacks of vegetables suspended from a pole carried on his shoulders, and return the next day. "He was a good farmer, and a cordial host," recalled U. E. Fries in his memoir *From Copenhagen to Okanogan*, "and this probably accounts for this town having been named after him."

He died around 1902.

No photograph of him exists.

Only this town bearing his name where recent rain had turned the hillsides soft lichen green, and mountains rumpled the horizon, more humped than jagged, and yellow aspens quivered among dark pockets of pines, and seeps spread in low swales where cows and horses stood in pairs and threes, chewing grass.

I arrived in Chesaw and headed straight to the graveyard: small, yes, and sick with spindly dry weeds, but with a brand-new fence of black iron or fake black iron with the spear-like points atop, as though to protect the graves from marauding intruders. An artfully crafted iron cowboy stood in silhouette against one bar, his hat tipped low. I pulled the gate open and walked into the space. Headstones, over-large, black with mold, leaned off-kilter and reached back a hundred years or more, well into Chee Saw's era. One, featuring a mini-temple with rooflines curving upwards, a style that could be construed as Chinese, was nameless. Several other gravestones were just that: stones, also nameless. One of these graves could be Chee Saw's. Hell, they could be anyone's.

I loitered much longer than I'd planned to. Why? What did I expect? That I'd scratch away rust-mold and see the name of the man for whom the town was named? Would this be too much to ask? Shouldn't a town's namesake deserve as much or better? I didn't need Chee Saw to have his own movie or kid-friendly biography or even a historical marker along the highway. I just wanted him to have a stone. The same way all these white men and women and children—my people—have stones in this place, in this ground, protected ridiculously by a spear-topped iron fence. But no. After an hour reading weather-worn names I left with socks full of stickers, seeds of invasive weeds, but nothing of Chee Saw. The injustice weighed on me like the layers of photocopies piled in manila folders beside my desk where I'd first considered the question.

Could Chee Saw and Ah Chee be the same person?

Chee Saw appears only once in written accounts before he arrived at Myers Creek. The year was 1868, so he was ten years younger, and unmarried, presumably, when he ran into a drove of cattle heading north from Walla Walla and joined up, offering to help any way he could. The man at the helm, Dan Drumheller, who would later become the largest cattle rancher in Eastern Washington, gauged him to be a top-notch hand, a daring horseman who could "handle a rope like a Mexican"—a compliment, apparently, and a rare nod to the Mexicans who roamed the territory in much fewer numbers than the Chinese but roamed it still.

Chee Saw and Drumheller headed north through Moses Coulee, past villages and gardens thriving, past other cattle drivers, too, along the busy trail bisecting black basalt cliffs. When they reached the Columbia River, the crossing proved treacherous, the water wilder and the cattle feistier than Drumheller had expected, and that's where Chee Saw proved himself indispensable. He was quick-thinking and quick-moving. If not for him, every last one of the animals would've drowned. Instead, they all made it across alive. Chee Saw saved the day. But he'd go no further. One steer, too, refused to continue with the herd. Drumheller left Chee Saw with his gratitude and the gift of a fine stubborn steer, right there along the Columbia River, near the confluence with the Okanogan River.

Where, according to Drumheller, Chee Saw happened to own a store.

I'd never heard of a store at the mouth of the Okanogan River. Never saw one on a map. It could've been a very small business or a short-lived one. Some "stores" in settler accounts are little more than shoddy lean-tos with scant supplies. This could've been one. Who knows?

On my way to Chesaw, I'd stopped at the spot to check it out. I pulled over and walked to a bluff and looked down at the wide flat confluence of the two rivers, the Columbia and the Okanogan, not so much colliding as splicing together, streams threading through sandbars and bisecting green willow-thick islands. Fort Okanogan, which consists of this overlook and a small museum, used to be managed by the Washington State Parks Department but was recently handed over to the Confederated Tribes of the Colville Reservation. A tribal representative worked nearby, pulling invasive weeds. She brushed her hands on the front of her jeans and offered one in greeting. We stood in a brisk autumn wind and marveled at the view and the luck of good working weather so late in the season. Finally she asked why I'd come.

"Have you ever heard of a Chinese store near the mouth of the Okanogan?" I asked.

She shook her head immediately, not the least uncertain.

"There were two forts," she said, "both started by fur trading companies in the early nineteenth century, and abandoned by 1860."

She pointed me toward two viewfinders through which you could look to see flagpoles at the sites of those forts, flooded since the 1960s by Wells Dam a few miles downstream.

"What about Chee Saw? The guy the town up north was named for? Ever heard of him?"

She'd never heard of him, nor the town of Chesaw, though she knew there'd been plenty of Chinese miners in the area. Some accounts told of gold miners stripping the abandoned fur station of lumber, leaving the site barren by 1880. But a Chinese store? She doubted it.

"The mining didn't really come this far upriver," she explained. "There'd be no clientele for a store."

If Chee Saw owned a store, she argued, it would've been downriver fifteen miles or so.

Closer to, say, Chelan Falls.

I could find no hard proof that Ah Chee, the merchant at Chelan Falls, and Chee Saw were the same man. No journal entry, no newspaper clipping, no hearsay, even. But there was also no Chinese store where Drumheller placed it, and I knew Ah Chee was a horseman. Nearly every description of the

Chinese merchant mentions his forty-horse pack string, and how, at least in the early days, he'd run the horses regularly to Walla Walla for supplies. Ah Chee would've been making the trek through Moses Coulee in 1868 at exactly the time when Drumheller appeared looking for a cowhand.

Say, for the sake of argument, that it was the same man: Chee Saw, Ah Chee. Why might Ah Chee sign on with Drumheller? Maybe he needed money or protection on the route north. Maybe he could use company. Whatever the reason, they'd travel for days through Moses Coulee and Ah Chee would surely prove his worth. He'd lived on the Columbia Plateau by then for years. He'd know where to find water, to hunt rabbit, to harvest serviceberries. He'd know which crops belonged to which Native people, which cattle drivers had a clue what the hell they were doing and which ones did not. He would've had the chance to bail on Drumheller, but he didn't. He stayed on the cattle drive until they reached the river. He saved a bunch of cattle from drowning, then chose to stay at his store.

Ah Chee stayed at the store at Chelan Falls until at least 1875 when the massacre occurred. Then, he moved on.

"The finances of the old Chinese merchant were running low," writes Steele in the 1906 history, "for he had grubstaked too many of his countrymen in their search for gold. In a big mine up on the Okanogan River he had an interest, and there he moved."

Ah Chee—or let's go ahead and call him Chee Saw—headed up the Okanogan.

The Okanogan Valley splays more broadly than those to the west. The mountains are wedged wider, a little like Alaska, and like Alaska, the place has an edge. Follow the Okanogan River north through Omak, Tonasket, and Oroville, and the vibe grows wilder, ever more self-sufficient, stubborn, out of the mainstream. If Chee Saw was trying to escape trouble, to duck under the radar, he'd fit right in today.

The Omak Stampede, an annual rodeo, boasts the world-famous Suicide Race. At the sound of a single gunshot, riders in life vests, many of them Native, charge their horses down a two-hundred-foot cliff-like hill or hill-like cliff into the river. Horses snap legs regularly. Animal rights groups protest. Crowds swarm. Twenty miles north in Tonasket, the annual Okanogan Family Barter Faire attracts thousands of people who'd rather, in principle, barter than spend. It's part organic grower's market, part costume festival, part communal campout. Drugs are prohibited; drugs are everywhere.

The ethic is common enough in the rural Northwest, this kind of cowboy-hippie-libertine exuberance, but it's more pointed in the Okanogan. There's a pervasive cheerful grating. Against norms. Against outsiders. Against the government.

Naturally, white separatists prosper. Northeastern Washington is not far from Ruby Ridge, Idaho, where twenty-five years ago an eleven-day standoff between white separatist Randy Weaver and FBI agents ended in the deaths of four people including two children, effectively starting the modern militia movement. Once, around that same era, Laurie and I traveled this way to buy some apple rootstock, a hearty winter variety, and the nursery owner greeted us—two young blond women—with overeager attention. He mentioned his sons often and listed their many qualities, solicitous as a horse trader. When we prepared to leave, he encouraged us to come again, to consider staying. They were looking, he said, for more people "like us."

If we'd come clean—said actually, we're not like you, not like you think—the mood would've changed, cooled considerably, though likely not turned dangerous. The code among white rural people is strong: live and let live. Avoid confrontation if possible. Our own adherence to the code was, in fact, probably why we didn't say anything. This is why the government makes such an excellent scapegoat. The government is nameless, distant, not someone you shake hands with, not someone who walks with you among the heirloom varieties as you point out your strapping son on the tractor out in the pasture in the sun.

Some say Chesaw is the edgiest place of all. When I talked to people about my visit before I left home, they'd smile. Be careful, they'd say. That's the kind of place where people go to get away from people, one said. Another friend told me all his Vietnam buddies went up there after their discharges. They holed up with drugs or guns or religion or nature and quiet, some combination of all of the above.

Chee Saw came in search of riches or to escape debtors. He came because he'd fallen hard in love and landed in the country of his beloved. Or maybe he was more calculating: using his Native wife to grab land fast. Or maybe he fell into the place the way anyone does, no different than leaving California, graduating from college, taking a job sight unseen over the telephone, and camping in a pickers' camp in a rainstorm. Not every move has a clear motivation. Sometimes you just stumble into the right place at the right time. For Chee Saw, the right place happened to be 3.2 miles from the Canadian border.

Exactly 3.2 miles north of town, I stopped to gaze at distant yellow hills, softly rolling, and a blue sky with white clouds billowing. To my right, Myers Creek ran shallow, shaded by willows. Ahead of me: a row of mailboxes, side by side, were coated in heavy road dust. Beyond that: an easy inviting cross-country stroll to…a foreign country? That's what I wanted to see for myself: how easy would it be to cross? Would it have been easy for Chee Saw? I rechecked my odometer. This had to be the place. But there was no sign other than "No Trespassing." It would take nothing to cross. Just park the car and take a stroll. In the age of ICE and drones, I was not about to risk it.

Instead I turned back toward town. Though some people had described Chesaw as a ghost town, the place, though small, seemed near-bustling to me. There was a community center, a fire hall, a grocery store, and a dozen houses, some with flower gardens. Rodeo grounds the size of a baseball field sat in the middle of town across from a tavern with a high wooden western-style false front and neon beer signs: Bud, Bud Light, MGD. Outside, a small group of men and women in hoodies smoked cigarettes. They were having a loud conversation, possibly an altercation, so I hesitated, fiddling with my phone, which had no reception anyway. I was at least a five-hour drive from any US city with more than one hundred thousand residents. There may have been some closer in British Columbia, but first you'd have to find the border. I figured someone at the Chesaw Tavern ought to be able to tell me where it was.

When I entered, the woman behind the bar asked if I wanted lunch and scrambled for a menu.

"No, no," I said. "Just a beer. Rainier?"

She nodded. I handed her four bills for the three-dollar bottle and considered asking about the border whereabouts, but it'd be hard for me to be heard over the only other mid-afternoon patron, a red-faced man in a black vest and cowboy boots, who ranted loudly to the empty room about the lack of women in town. He met one, he says, but turned out she was just visiting from Tacoma. He spit out the city name, Tacoma, like venom. I imagined he was the reason everyone else was smoking in the parking lot. I asked the bartender if I could take my beer outside.

"Out back," she said and lifted her chin toward a dark hallway, as though hoping the ranter wouldn't notice. He didn't.

Outside, a high fence surrounded a small lawn with three empty picnic tables. An older man worked alone, fixing a gate. Eight or ten feet long, the gate sagged so it couldn't swing open. He had a jack to hold up one side and a two-by-four to tack across diagonally. He also had an old hand drill, a brace-and-bit, exactly the kind I used on trail crew. I sat watching the sky, that amazing sky, and admiring the brace-and-bit and the gumption it takes to make the tool work. I watched the man drill a hole at shoulder height, then rest.

"I can do the bottom one," I said. "It can be hard to get down on your knees, I know."

"Sure," he said. "Getting down is not a problem, but getting back up is."

He went looking for a longer lag screw while I drilled. When he returned, I ratcheted the new lag in place. The whole procedure took four minutes and made me unreasonably happy. Away from the ranting man, away from the smoking clique, Chesaw seemed like a nice place. The man told me he and his wife owned the tavern and the store. They bought it when he retired fourteen years earlier, lost it in the recession, and just recently got it back. I thought I could get another beer and ask for the rest of the story. Instead I got right to the point:

"Where's the border, exactly?"

"Three point two miles north," he said. The stock answer.

"What's there?"

He took the socket wrench and rechecked the lag screw I had just tightened to make sure it was tight.

"You can't drive across," he said. "Only Midway or Oroville, and Midway closes at five, so you'd better get going."

I had no plans to hurry across the border, but didn't say as much. I fiddled with my empty beer bottle, wondering if there was a recycle bin. I wanted to press the point: What if I just started walking? How hard would it be? But felt ridiculously fearful that asking would label me, put me under surveillance. Someone might think I planned to smuggle drugs or terrorists. I'm not usually afraid of the government. I worked for a federal agency for half my adult life. I happily pay my taxes. But still. I decided not to ask anything more. Once paranoia takes root, it's hard to shake.

I tossed the bottle in the trash and slipped out the new gate, swinging free.

*

In the late 1800s, the Syilx Okanagan people didn't care a whit about the border. The Native people knew their tule mat dwellings on one side of the invisible line were no different than the ones on the other. The salmon, the grizzlies, the berries, all the same. The rituals, the language, the relatives. Same. Newly arrived United States Army officials chose their battles with Native people carefully, and border security wasn't one of them. No one cared if Syilx Okanagan people crossed the border. They only cared if Chinese people did.

By 1880, over one hundred thousand Chinese people lived in the United States, 99 percent of them in the West, and anti-Chinese fervor had begun to roil. Newspaper cartoons showed the so-called celestials as hideous creatures, menacing slant-eyed intruders, and editorials oozed hate, some of the worst of it in Olympia, Tacoma, and Seattle. As a result of incessant pestering from westerners—and the omnipresent threat of violence—politicians in Washington, DC, reluctantly passed the Chinese Exclusion Act. There were loopholes and exceptions put in place by distant globally-minded politicians and more secretly by local business owners desperate to keep cheap labor. But the fact was, by 1882, only four years after Chee Saw's arrival at Myers Creek, any Chinese person who wanted to cross from Canada into the United States was going to have a hell of a time.

Oh, they found ways. Some sneaked through in canoes and skiffs. They braved the cross-currents and tides of the Salish Sea, played hide-and-seek through the maze of islands, the Canadian Gulf Islands and Washington's San Juans indistinguishable for the most part. Some got caught and sent right back across, until Canada began to charge a head tax for immigrants entering their country, and if these new sea-soaked Chinese immigrants—who had been Canadian emigrants just hours before—couldn't pay the tax, they were sent right back to the United States where they'd be imprisoned without a charge and held indefinitely. The first case of indefinite migrant detention in the United States of America, but not the last.

Not just newcomers got hassled. If you were a Chinese person living in Washington Territory, even if you'd been here for decades, and you traveled abroad, back to China, say, or to Canada where you happened to have relatives or a part-time job in a sawmill, you'd have to show paperwork to get back in. Hardly anyone had the proper paperwork. The Salish Sea became the site of a long-running game of cat-and-mouse, which fueled anti-Chinese sentiments all the more.

Meanwhile, on the dry empty side of the Cascades, four hundred miles of so-called border were guarded by one lone officer. In the place soon to be named Chesaw, you could waltz right across on foot or on a horse on a trail that'd been used by miners and cattlemen for half a century, and by Native people for eons before that, a trail that followed Myers Creek, the very same Myers Creek along which Chee Saw built his log home. By happenstance or design, he'd found the ideal spot.

"When the Chinese Exclusion Act of 1882 restricted Chinese coming into the USA," one history explains, "a lucrative smuggling trade from Canada was expanded to include Chinese miners and their sporting substance opium. The Chinese were transported to the border crossing like the one near Lake Osoyoos, and slipped into US gold fields." (Illegal immigrants. Illegal drugs. A too-familiar refrain.) Not just opium, but laudanum, too, which was widely used as a cure-all by "cow punches and farming women, alike. It was just a darn good medicine to them, and yes, it could cure a hangover."

Maybe smuggling wasn't the only business Chee Saw engaged in, but it's hard to imagine he didn't do some.

The next morning in a heavy drizzle, I crossed the border myself and found, unsurprisingly, that for a white woman in 2017 to drive across the border at an official port of entry with a US passport in a Honda SUV is a breeze. At first, much remained the same. The wedged-wide mountains, the pines, and the grasses: the same. Even the libertarian vibe, at first: the same. Frequent hand-painted signs reading "No National Park" lined the fences. The government of British Columbia and the Syilx Okanagan Nation had proposed a new park reserve, which opponents claimed threatened private property rights, cattle grazing, and local sovereignty. (Another familiar refrain.) But soon the edge smoothed off. Speed limits lowered. Fruit stands offered late-season tomatoes, garlic, and squash. Wineries abounded. Signs announced a ski gear swap at the curling rink at Penticton, and I considered stopping. When I grabbed coffee in Kelowna, I overheard conversations in at least three languages. Already, the place felt more cosmopolitan and, well, more civilized than the US.

Canada, for many Americans, represents the ultimate fallback plan. "Guess we'll have to move to Canada" becomes the mantra of the government-friendly when the government isn't to our liking. ("Have at it!" cry opponents.) It seems an ironic instinct, the flipside of xenophobia—"when things get rough, become an immigrant" as opposed to "when things get rough, blame immigrants"—and it's one I've avoided in large part because the chances of even Canadians welcoming a half-broke writer with no tech training are nearly zilch.

But Chee Saw? Why wouldn't he just cross and stay?

That question led me north past Lake Osoyoos on a highway skirting Lake Okanagan, a super-sized version of Lake Chelan. The mountains grew steeper and more forested. Clouds hung dense white at mid-elevation and wrapped like thick swathes of fabric around the dark slopes. Kelowna, 130 kilometers north of the border, once boasted a sizeable Chinatown. On the day I planned my visit, the local Okanagan Heritage Museum featured a rotating exhibit on Chinese gold miners.

Here, for the first time, I found the mid-nineteenth-century gold rush characterized as the first great international migration, wherein hundreds of thousands of rural Chinese migrants filtered out into the world, heading first to San Francisco, then to Melbourne, then to British Columbia, reshaping the world's population as they did. But it didn't last long. Within a few short decades, the gold in British Columbia's Fraser Valley had played out. The railroad was built. As in the US, the economic squeeze was on. Employers didn't need the cheap labor like they once did.

So the Canadians, like the Americans, started to pass laws against the Chinese.

The laws, according to the Canadian government itself, denied basic human rights including "the right to vote, to hold public office, or own property; imposed labor, educational, and employment restrictions, subjected them to health and housing segregation, and prevented them from participating fully in society." The details are laid bare in an official apology penned by the legislative assembly of British Columbia on May 14, 2014, which goes on to state: "The House deeply regrets that these Canadians were discriminated against simply because they were of Chinese descent." The motion, framed on the wall at the Kelowna exhibit, acknowledges the "overwhelming contributions" of Chinese Canadians and expresses the government's purpose clearly: to ensure this never happens again.

The apology is the kind of thing you see more rarely in the United States—the national historic site at Manzanar where Japanese Americans were interned during World War II comes to mind—and it's hard to know what difference an official apology makes, but as I stood alone in the museum on a rainy morning, it made me hopeful.

On the way back home, I made one last stop for lunch in Oroville, Washington, ten miles south of the border. Named for gold—oro—whatever small fortune the northernmost American town in the Okanogan Valley made was not in gold, but in a more pedestrian product: tomatoes. Or so I learned at the tiny Depot Museum just off the main highway through town, three blocks from the diner, where the docent, Arnie Marchand, made eager conversation. I'd left my burger sitting in the car, getting cold and soggy, but Arnie was not going to let me slip out after a sneak peek. A congenial gray-haired man, he wore a black shirt buttoned to the neck. A fleece jacket and his briefcase sitting beside him attested to his membership in the Confederated Tribes of the Colville Reservation. In an enlarged black-and-white photo sitting directly in front of his docent's desk, a group of men stood in a circle, their arms crossed, their faces resigned and furious. Arnie watched me study the photo while he served up a steady stream of small talk. Usually, he said, they get hundreds of visitors a day at the Depot Museum, but nearby wildfires have kept crowds at bay. Plus the season was nearing its end.

"Today it's been eleven," he said and clicked the counter on his desk. "Twelve, with you."

"What's going on in the picture?" I asked.

Arnie nodded. He'd been waiting for this. "That's the day Grand Coulee drowned our river," he said.

"The dam."

He nodded again. "It was bad enough the traditional fishing grounds at Kettle Falls were lost, but hundreds of burial sites were, too. We weren't even given warning."

"It was tragic," I said.

"That's the government for you," he said.

Much of the rest of the room had been decorated with fruit labels: apples, mostly, some tomatoes, and since the building was a former train depot, there was some railroad paraphernalia. A dummy dressed in a train conductor's cap and striped shirt faced out the window. In another room, three mannequins posed in a faux one-room schoolhouse. On a side wall, a mishmash of artifacts—beaded gloves, a headdress, baskets—were displayed in a glass case. On loan, Arnie said, without apparent irony, from the museum at Grand Coulee Dam.

I asked about Chee Saw, and Arnie said he didn't know much.

"I have an eighty-year-old friend, she loves this stuff. I could call her. She'll come right over."

"Thanks, but I'm on a tight schedule. I have a ferry to catch."

I paged through a few documents, checked my watch, and made a move to leave. Only then did he point out a book on the sale shelf that bore his name, *The Way I Heard It*, a collection of regional tales—true and tall, ancient and modern, short and folksy. I ran to the car for a twenty and had him sign a copy.

"What about the massacre?" I asked. "At Chelan Falls? Have you ever heard of that?"

"Yeah," he said. He grinned mischievously. "They were all in here, those Chinamen, and so we killed them. Hundreds, everywhere. It was our land, all of it, and down there at Chelan Falls? We killed maybe seven hundred of them."

"Seven hundred?"

I didn't believe him. No source I'd seen came anywhere close to a number that large.

"At least," he said.

"Why?" I asked.

Arnie explained how the Chinese mined the gold and built the railroads, and then it was over and they had nowhere to go.

"There were laws, good laws, to take care of the problem," he said. "But they didn't follow them. Just like now."

I had no reply to that.

"That's the government for you," he said.

PART II:
NOT VOICES EXACTLY

Chapter Seven
MASSACRE: VERSION II

The attackers gather at dawn in Chelan, an almost-town, a row of ramshackle wood-front buildings well away from the camp where three years after the big quake the spewing sulfurous springs have finally quieted. The men shed their suits, pass tins of shoe polish—or gunpowder or the crushed hulls of black walnuts—to stain their raw fresh-shaven cheeks, and walk, rather than ride, toward the Columbia. They trudge past Beebe Springs, scoop cold water in their palms to drink, climb a rocky treeless ravine. They can see the Chinese store across the river, and as they creep nearer they see women, children by their sides, tending rows of squash. But they can't see the river itself. The drop is too steep, too close. They won't see the river until it's over.

The Wanapum Heritage Center sits alongside the Columbia River one hundred miles south of Chelan Falls near Priest Rapids Dam. To get there you follow I-90, the interstate that runs east from green lush Seattle over the Cascades into wide dry country: Spokane, then Montana and the Dakotas, on to Chicago and points beyond. Along the road, the land stretches flat and brown except for where the dams soak green crops, some now labeled by fence-mounted signs: alfalfa, corn, wheat. Take a right and follow a two-lane highway south along the river. Now the land folds upward: mesas and canyons, stark and eroded, a source of solace or desolation, depending on your tolerance for aridity or your state of mind on a given day.

On the morning I arrived, swipes of clouds crisscrossed the autumn sky. No signs announced Archaeology Days, but plenty of people apparently knew to come. At nine sharp, the parking lot was full. I pulled into a makeshift gravel lot cordoned off for the event and near hay bales where I'd watch a spear-throwing demonstration later in the day.

Ever since I started asking questions about the Chelan Falls massacre, a second theory about the attackers has festered. Every written source, except one, attributes the murders to Native men. Maybe Chelan, maybe Methow. In person, though, I'd heard another version from Sue and Dave Clouse, and more recently from Keith Carpenter, the grandson of early settlers, who told me how growing up he heard the story both ways.

"Might've been white guys," he said. "There's no way to know."

I wrote an email to *Native River* author William Layman, who quotes a later Chinese merchant, Que Yu, saying he heard white men committed the atrocity. I asked Layman about his source, which I'd been trying to track down in libraries and archives around the region. He did not remember precisely where he found the documents, but out of the blue he invited me to meet him at Archaeology Days. A friend of his, Colville Confederated tribal member Randy Lewis (Kay'axən), would be in attendance, too, he said, and Randy would know more.

Archaeology is not my field of expertise. My closest association came when I worked in the backcountry for the National Park Service. In those days, we'd occasionally need to check with archaeologists before disturbing the dirt to build a camp, say, or a new stretch of trail. When we did, we turned to Bob Mierendorf. Though he'd likely reject the label, Mierendorf is a living legend. When I started work at North Cascades National Park in the early 1990s, the stock narrative, espoused in print and enshrined on visitor center displays, claimed that Indigenous people had only ever "passed through" the mountains. They never stayed. A claim that, even then, seemed ignorant or evasive or, at best, incomplete. When Bob Mierendorf starting surveying the back-country as a graduate student in 1984, there were seventeen sites identified in the nearly eight-hundred-thousand-acre park. By the time he retired as park archaeologist in 2013, he'd identified more than three hundred, including more than forty at high elevation. In other words, Indigenous people had used the mountains all the time. Of course they had.

At Wanapum Heritage Center, I discovered that Archaeology Days consisted of two days of crafts and education for kids followed by one more day—this day—with more formal conference-style archaeology presentations. The Wanapum people, who've inhabited this stretch of river for millennia, sponsor the event, which began in the 1990s and had recently moved into this fifty-thousand-square-foot facility built for and with the Wanapum community by the Grant County Public Utility District as mitigation for the damage dams have done. By mid-morning, I was sitting under high ceilings in a brightly lit room, listening to a presentation way beyond my grasp, riddled with acronyms and numbered labeling systems for artifacts, getting embarrassingly sleepy. At a break between sessions, I stood to stretch and noticed Bob Mierendorf sitting right in front of me.

I should've known he'd be here. More to the point, I should have thought of contacting him about the massacre. Of all the people I knew, he'd be the most likely to know about pre-settler history. Or, in this case, early settler history. I was eager to learn what he knew, but we only had a few minutes to make small talk before Bill Layman and Randy Lewis were to start their presentation. As we retook our seats, my mind wandered back in time.

I met Bob Mierendorf on the same day I first spied the North Cascades. I'd been living in Seattle and on the weekend took a long drizzly drive up the Skagit River to visit a friend who was living with her boyfriend, a Native skills enthusiast. Turned out they shared a rental house with several park employees: a geologist, a carpenter, a dispatcher, and Bob Mierendorf. The boyfriend was tanning a deer hide in the basement with canoe paddles and a bucket of deer brains, slow stinky work, and I decided to help him. For my help, the boyfriend gave me an atlatl, an ancient spear-throwing tool he'd made, painstakingly, from deer hide, bone, sinew, and local cedar. I thought it was the most generous gift I'd ever been given, and when I left in the late afternoon, the clouds lifted and I saw the dramatic snowy peaks on the horizon, and I knew somehow my life had changed, sure as tectonic plates shifting under my feet. I had no idea that in less than a year I'd be camping at Beebe Bridge preparing to move to the mountains.

Bill Layman and Randy Lewis stood to speak, and I was relieved to hear their jargon-free style—tag-teaming perspectives on pictographs near Rock Island, the site of the first dam on the Columbia, and a longtime sacred site for the Native people who traveled past. It was a lively showcase, fascinating, and I was taken by their easy banter with one another. I spoke to them afterward briefly, but we were interrupted in the scramble to find seats for lunch, which would be free, Bill informed me, and something of a feast. In the hullabaloo, I lost track of Randy entirely.

I began to realize Archaeology Days was more homecoming than conference. The atmosphere was both casual and exuberant, a celebration of the place and its people. Wanapum elders, we were told, would fill their plates first. Before they did, a dozen or so were each given a chance to speak. Folding tables were lined tightly, more than the room should probably have held, and the elders stood from their seats, dressed more colorfully than the guests—two hundred or so land agency managers, academics, field workers, and curious locals for whom soft hikers and clean blue jeans were the norm. The elders, nearly all women, were unhurried with the microphone, and each of them thanked us for coming as if this were a family reunion. Together we bowed our heads for a blessing before lining up for food. Venison stew, salmon, fry bread with jam, coleslaw, salad, cake, and more.

The church picnic vibe remained strong. Hostess-frantic women with thick forearms handled steaming ladles. Men with spatulas served salmon from wide baking trays. I was waiting my turn, standing in the bright white-walled hallway, when a man behind me elbowed me gently.

Randy Lewis is a tall man, more than a foot taller than me, quick-witted, with a disconcertingly steady gaze, warm and skeptical at once. Google him, and you learn he's a veteran of the American Indian rights movement of the 1970s, a participant in the occupation of Alcatraz, an author, and a dedicated keeper of oral tradition along the Columbia River. Meet him in person, and you get straight-talk.

"What do you know about the Chelan Falls massacre?" I asked.

"You mean that time when the white guys dressed up like Indians?"

I nodded uncertainly. "Do you know where exactly it happened?"

"Over by the springs," he said. He described the pullout where I'd walked near Beebe Springs, the ones that appeared after the 1872 earthquake. Not where Dave Clouse's friend fell. Not a location anyone else ever mentioned. But one that made a lot of sense. The bluff is high enough, and the water from the new geyser spraying into the air would be worth fighting for.

"And so it was white guys that did it?"

"Yes," he said. No hesitance whatsoever.

I looked at his expression for context or elaboration. He looked neither angry nor amused, not sad nor boastful. He was simply stating the truth, and he expected me to accept it.

"They always say it was Indians, a couple of Chelans were put in jail, but that's not what happened."

I had never heard of anyone going to jail.

He told me his great-uncle, as a boy, overheard a group of white men—some of them men for whom streets in Chelan are still named—bragging about the murders in a corner tavern. This would've been years after the actual event, the town grown larger. I pictured the boy pushing a broom over rough-sawn floorboards or washing dishes in a steel bin, unnoticed or not worth noticing, as drunk men in suit coats lean back to crow loudly.

"You know that tavern?" Randy asked.

We were holding overfull paper plates of food and holding up the line, too.

"I do," I said.

He nodded as if that sealed the deal, and he walked away.

After lunch, I skipped the presentations and instead watched demonstrations on the patio outside. Flint knapping, basket-making, weaving, atlatl throwing. At the most popular one, three men tanned a deer hide the old-fashioned way with brains and a bone scraper, much the same way my friend's boyfriend had done. An older man in an elegant wool vest and a white collared shirt explained the process while two young men in sweaty T-shirts did the actual work. A small crowd gathered to ask questions. How soft it gets. How much time it takes. The practice, the patience, and the smell especially, reminded me of that visit to the Skagit so many years ago, and of Bob Mierendorf, too. Where had he gone? In my eagerness to speak with Randy, I'd forgotten to ask if Bob knew anything about the massacre.

I found him in the lobby and asked. Oh, he'd heard the story alright, and not only that, he worked on the archaeological survey of the Chinese store area at Beebe Bridge in the late 1980s. He didn't remember finding many artifacts.

"But there was something," Bob said, nodding thoughtfully. He called out to a woman I will call Vicki standing in the crowded lobby, an old friend of his who had worked on the Beebe Bridge project with him. He explained my interest in the massacre and asked if she remembered the dig.

"Yes, yes," she said. She answered breathlessly, almost nervously. "In fact, it was the strangest thing…"

They were doing test excavations, she explained. These pits are usually one meter square, but Bob wanted to be more precise, so he had them dig fifty centimeters by fifty centimeters, which made the job more challenging. Their heads would be down in this tiny hole, and as she was digging, alone in her assigned area, she kept feeling a presence, like hearing the sounds someone makes when approaching, tools jangling or footsteps. She'd come up and look around and not see anyone.

"I don't remember hearing voices," she said. "Not exactly."

At some point she decided enough is enough and just sat waiting.

"Something made me think of the Chinese. Maybe one of the landowners had mentioned them and alluded to trouble but I certainly hadn't heard about the massacre. Not back then. I learned about it much later."

"Did you feel spooked?" I asked.

"Yes," she said. "That is the word for it."

Later when I followed up on the phone, she told me how she'd done tons of solo hiking and camping in a life spent outdoors, and had never felt anything like this anywhere else before or after. In the moment, in the bustling lobby of the Wanapum Heritage Center, she paused, and then added one more detail.

"The thing is, it felt like children. You know the way kids like to romp? It felt like a child ran by. That brush or breeze."

"Children?" I asked.

She nodded. The conversation flagged.

Her story was too chilling, too hard to process, so we retreated to easier territory: where exactly were they? Bob believed it was closer to the store, though Vicki disagreed, and she had no patience for guessing games. She pulled up Google Earth on her phone and pointed to an alluvial fan protruding into the river north of the bridge, now covered in orchards, a place not mentioned in any version of the story I'd heard. It was on the far side of the river from the location Dave and Sue Clouse and I picked out. It was, in fact, on the *opposite* side of the river from where every single existing description places the massacre. Almost directly across from Beebe Springs where Randy Lewis said the massacre occurred.

She said she was 100 percent sure that's where they were.

As we talked, Randy Lewis passed by, heading toward the patio where the last of afternoon sunlight reflected off steady ripples on the river. I reached out to touch his arm.

"Randy. Wait. Which side of the river did you say the massacre was on again?"

"Well, actually both sides," he said. "Right there by the springs, and also across the river. They killed the men on one side, and the women and children on the other side."

I was stunned. Not one account of the massacre had suggested massacres on two sides of the river. None mentioned women and children. Randy had never met Vicki. There was no way he could have overheard our conversation in the crowded lobby.

When we described Vicki's experience to him, he nodded solemnly as if to say: of course.

Randy Lewis was the only one among us completely unsurprised that the truth might be radically different from any story we'd been told.

*

And so the attackers approach. They ferry across the river in the predawn dark, oars splashing gently, and stash their boat among willows far from shore. They watch the women spread out into the fields, obscured among the cornstalks, stooped beside beans, kneeling in squash vines, children by their sides. The men crouch in a patch of serviceberry as the sun rises and the infernal wind begins to howl. As they wait for the signal from the others on the high bluff across the river, they listen to riffles over stone, and the wind down the canyon like voices, like children laughing, or the whisper when they pass close.

Chapter Eight
XENOPHOBIA TAKES ROOT

Outside the window of our cabin in Stehekin sits a burn barrel. Literally, a barrel to burn stuff in. A friend gave it to us when we first bought the land. Fashioned from a section of steel diversion pipe at the local hydro plant, it once drew water from a creek to a powerhouse, through a turbine, to run our lights. Now it barbecues our burgers. Our friend salvaged the steel, welded on a bottom plate, and personalized it, too, with uneven welded-on letters. "The Homestead," it reads alongside the date we moved in. It was a generous gift, one we've used exuberantly—roasting veggies, burning scrap lumber, warming our hands in winter. But when I read the welded words these days, I feel uneasy.

The truth is the label never sat right with me. We're not homesteaders, not really, not even settlers. *Settled* isn't the right word for the way we stumbled into the place, the same way anyone does: because we had jobs here. We came to work, and work we did. We worked physically during the day. I lugged a chainsaw up steep switchbacks to clear logs or used a brush whip to knock back ferns and nettles, loppers for the harder-stemmed plants: boxwood, serviceberry, wild cherry. Laurie pruned apple trees, grafted them, cleared irrigation ditches, built fences. At home we worked more. We hauled rocks from the ditch we dug with a backhoe for plumbing and electricity, and saved the ones flat on two sides to rock-face the foundation, a job that took more than ten years. The list could go on. The work was, and is sometimes still, a matter of pride and a source of identity, and a way to justify ourselves. We worked, and by working, we belonged.

"They worked hard," reads one account of Chinese miners along the Columbia River in the late 1800s. "They were quiet, honest, dependable, and therefore were treated most abominably, worse than Indians."

The upside-down world: because they worked hard, the Chinese did not belong.

Start with their appearance. Loose-fitting clothes, a shaved forehead with a long braid—the queue originally forced upon them by Manchu rulers. White men claimed they looked, frankly, girlish. (Their exclusion would lead the way for the exclusion of homosexuals starting in 1917.) They claimed loose clothes hid cash or gold.

They called them celestials.

"The phrase 'celestial empire,' meaning more or less 'empire ruled in accord with Heaven,' goes back a long way in China," Chuimei Ho, editor of the Chinese in Northwest America Research Committee (CINARC) website, explained to me via email. "But it wasn't until the early nineteenth century that English and French translations began to appear in foreign publications and even Chinese diplomatic correspondence." The plural, Ho suggests, may have been introduced innocently by journalists who wanted to spice up their writing with a colorful synonym.

But here's the rub: "The usage quickly became pejorative when readers interpreted it as meaning that Chinese, absurdly in view of their obviously inferior economic and legal status, considered themselves to be superior to ordinary humans," she continued. "Calling a mere laundryman 'celestial' was an irony that even the least educated anti-Chinese white hoodlum could understand."

Irony as the realm of the racist apparently goes back long

before the internet. So too the idea that the oppressed are uppity. They think they're better than us and therefore deserve our disdain.

Accounts of the Chinese community along the Columbia River in the 1880s—all written by white people—lean hard on the kind of broad sweeping generalizations you can only make when no one's around to refute them. The authors recount stories they heard from their fathers or grandfathers or maybe around a barrel stove in a tavern. With tiny seeds of truth, they're nevertheless full of hyperbole and derision on familiar themes. Chinese people were addicts. "They took opium every two weeks, then slept for two weeks," reads one. "Then they'd wake and work for two weeks." They were disloyal aliens who sneaked untold riches and even body parts back to China. "That's why there are no Chinamen in the graveyards."

Whether Chee Saw used opium we can't know, but if he did, he certainly didn't sleep for two weeks or he would've lost his inventory straightaway. If he sent money back to China, he can't be accused of squirreling away his fortune overseas. His store is often cited as the first successful business in the region; merchandise he sold drove development. If a white man started two or five businesses in the territory, no one would care if his profits ended up in Pennsylvania or Scotland or Timbuktu. It's hard to imagine a white man's ethnicity would be noticed at all if the nine-hundred-page 1906 *History of North Central Washington* is any guide. In nearly five hundred profiles of famous settlers—all men, all white, some with immigrant-seeming names like Bjork or Holzhauser—ethnicity is hardly ever mentioned. Wapato John, one of few Native men profiled, is noted for being "a devoted member of the Catholic church who never took part in uprisings and was always raising his voice for peace." As for the location of Chee Saw's remains? Well, there's no saying.

To be fair, many homespun descriptions are less overtly racist, even occasionally sympathetic, though they tended to the kind of coolie-esque romanticism of workers that could easily breed pity. "They were sometimes contracted," reads one, "sometimes bought, sometimes kidnapped, and made about 15 cents a day, seven days a week, and still sent money home to their families." The story told most often is that the Chinese miners moved in and took over mining claims after the white miners gave up and because they were harder workers, whether genetically programmed or psychologically trained to be tougher, the whole race of them, through sheer doggedness, found gold dust the whites had missed.

Maybe the Chinese miners worked harder than the whites— or some did and some didn't as is the way of all work, all workers, everywhere—but that's not why they found more gold. One reason they did: better technology. In "No Need to Rush: The Chinese, Placer Mining, and the Western Environment," Liping Zhu explains Guangdong, the Pearl River region where most of the miners came from, was heavily dependent on irrigation. People who farmed there were masters of hydraulic engineering, and they brought their technology, the knowledge at least, with them. The ubiquitous rocker, for example, was like a miniature rocking horse, a board with riffles across it, coated in quicksilver. Miners could pour buckets of gravel in water over the contraption, rock it back and forth, and gold dust, attracted by the quicksilver, stopped at the riffles. The rocker was simple, elegant, ingenious, and was eventually adopted by placer miners all over the world. But you couldn't use it alone. It required at least two people, preferably four.

So there's another reason they found gold: cooperation. The Chinese miners had to work together. No self-sufficiency, no rugged individualism. The every-man-for-himself dudes had already given up. Another, even more efficient gadget, called a Long Tom, required miners to saw boards from driftwood, then build a sluice, a three-sided box, ten to sixteen feet long, and set it on a slanted scaffold. Same theory as the rocker, but you needed ten or twenty men to pour water into the Long Tom. Ten or twenty men working together. It's possible these were *Survivor*-style alliances of strategy or convenience that could crack under pressure at any time, but that doesn't seem to have happened much, or at least the fractures weren't recorded.

And one more reason. Even though the Chinese men were so much smaller, they were, by all accounts, stronger than white men. Zhu argues the reason was better health. Chinese villages on the river each had a doctor, and some had two. They used herbs and knew how to use mold to treat infections a half-century before penicillin. Plus they had gardeners who grew vegetables in the blistering sun, the rocky glacial soil, so the Chinese miners ate greens—though the whites ridiculed the practice—and got plenty of vitamins and were stronger as a result.

What's absolutely true is this: Chinese people were doing the lion's share of work in the West. Not just on the railroad. Not just in laundries. Not just mining the gold dust dregs along the Columbia. By the late nineteenth century, some historians estimate, they were doing between half and three quarters of the farm labor in California. Chinese people were not taking over the country—they made up only 4 percent of immigrants to the US between 1870 and 1880—but they were working hard, and working itself became the source of scorn.

Xenophobia, a word with roots that appear ancient—from the Greek "xenos" for strange and "phobos" for fear—didn't register a first usage in English, according to *Merriam Webster*, until the 1880s, smack in the middle of anti-Chinese fervor. But mistrust and mistreatment of strangers started, of course, long before then and often focused on those doing the most menial labor. In the mid-1800s, the populist Know Nothing party arose as pro-labor, anti-Catholic, anti-immigrant, and anti-Irish in particular. They held forced raids in Boston, a town where the

Catholics had become 20 percent of the population, and they became wildly successful politically across the nation. In 1854, the Know Nothings took over eight governorships, nine state legislatures, and over one hundred seats in the House of Representatives. They won a few legislative victories—they lobbied for, and got, twenty-one-day waiting periods for naturalization of Irish immigrants—but their power didn't last long. Turns out, the Know Nothings were good at campaigning and rousing crowds, but lousy at governing, and other than restricting immigration, they shared few goals or values. Most glaringly, some were abolitionists, some were pro-slavery. The Civil War brought their downfall. Abraham Lincoln was pro-immigration, and by 1864 the Republicans had added a pro-immigration plank in their platform. Still, the Know Nothings had paved a road for anti-Chinese furor to follow.

If the rise of Chinese hate in the American West needs a villain, it's Denis Kearney. An immigrant himself from County Cork, Ireland, Kearney started the Workingmen's Party of California in the late 1870s in response to high unemployment. The aim was ostensibly to protect working people from exploitation, with party planks that called for an eight-hour workday and an end to subsidies for the railroad companies, but Kearney quickly turned his ire, and considerable charisma, on the people working hardest: the Chinese. He referred to them not merely as "celestials" but as "Asiatic pests" who carried infectious diseases. He stood in a vacant sandlot next to city hall in San Francisco day after day and gave speeches like screeds, growing louder and louder, until he stripped off his jacket and loosened his collar, and led the crowd in chanting, "The Chinese must go!" Reporters were quick to pick up the catchy refrain—a surefire way to sell papers—and at the end of 1876, twenty thousand residents of California signed a petition in favor of ousting Chinese immigrants lest the state become a "colony of China."

To be sure, anti-Chinese sentiment had simmered in California long before Kearney's rise to power. During the height of the gold run, the state had passed the Foreign Miners' Tax Act of 1850 that charged every miner who was not a US citizen a whopping twenty dollars a month per claim. Kearney raised the stakes. As he grew more popular, he began to explicitly incite violence, urging listeners to murder politicians or, more often, Chinese people in the name of national defense. "California must be all-American or all-Chinese," he cried. "We are resolved that it shall be American, and are prepared to make it so." He even called for a wall to be built along the southern border to keep Chinese people from sneaking into the US from Mexico.

Here's where my fierce loyalty to working people and those who fight for them takes a hard blow. So does my faith that since my ancestors (Irish, Italian, and German) were immigrants like the Chinese, they remain blameless in this particular mess. So many Irishmen and union workers joined the anti-Chinese movement that Kearney's followers were sometimes called the "Irish Know-Nothings." Kearney went after the robber barons and the elites, the press and the politicians, and the Chinese population right along with them. He took familiar stereotypes to their extremes until even the penchant for hard work got twisted into a sinister flaw. Early in his career he praised their "industriousness" but by the late 1870s, the same quality had turned to weakness. "They are imported by companies, controlled as serfs, worked like slaves, and at last go back to China with all their earnings."

The rhetoric took root. In the summer of 1877, rioters in San Francisco burned Chinese businesses, rampaged the wharves where steamers arrived with new Chinese immigrants aboard, and killed several Chinese men. From there the violence spread. The sheer volume and depravity is astounding. Between 1877 and 1890, according to CINARC, at least forty major acts of violence against Chinese people took place in the Pacific Northwest. Most occurred in Oregon, Washington, and Idaho, with one in British Columbia, and one in Juneau, Alaska. Nearly all were committed by white people, sometimes wearing masks. Sometimes the motive was greed or jealousy, especially of gold, yes, but the cruelty was more voracious than calculated. Chinese businesses were often burned—in Yreka, California, five Chinese children burned to death in one such fire—and people were forcibly removed at gunpoint or with ropes around their necks. In Juneau, more than one hundred Chinese men, women, and children were launched to sea without supplies. Tacoma famously forced out five hundred Chinese people overnight "peaceably" on November 4, 1885, though at least three people died along the way. In all, CINARC records 132 verifiable Chinese deaths during those years due to violence. Imagine how many went unrecorded.

To be clear, it's not as if the Chinese did not defend themselves. They did.

During the era in which Denis Kearney enjoyed his brief stint as a demagogue, he had a formidable nemesis. Writer and activist Wong Chin Foo used fanfare to expose Kearney's buffoonery. In 1883 in New York, he challenged Kearney to a duel with the choice of weapon: Irish potatoes, chopsticks, or a Krupp gun. Kearney declined and soon fell from favor almost as fast as he rose. Members of his Workingmen's Party marched through San Francisco in early 1880 demanding that factory owners fire all Chinese workers. Many complied—more than one thousand Chinese workers lost their jobs—but late the same year, the courts intervened. Nearly all anti-Chinese laws in California were overturned. Kearney ran for office and lost. By the end of the short decade, he'd slunk away into relative obscurity investing quietly in the stock market. He died a wealthy businessman of precisely the type he used to excoriate. Wong

Chin Foo started an association for Chinese American voters and the first Chinese American newspaper in the United States. Though his record is far from pure—he tended to favor upper-class Chinese Americans over laborers—he's often praised as a civil rights leader, the "Dr. Martin Luther King Jr. of Chinese Americans."

In Chelan Falls, after the massacre, a group of Chinese miners tried to enact their own revenge. The miners formed a makeshift army, a posse of sorts, to chase after their attackers, but they ran out of food. None of the white merchants would sell to them. You'd think white settlers would be eager to supply anyone willing to do the dirty work of harassing Native people. The fact that they weren't—that not a single white merchant was—lends some credence to the white-men-as-attackers version of the story.

If white men dressed up at Chelan Falls, they weren't the first to use the tactic. At the Boston Tea Party, whites dressed as Indigenous people to toss the crates into the harbor. Not so much to escape blame, but to make themselves distinct from the Brits. They took the mantle of "Native" with pride as though having landed on the continent and stayed a couple generations was the same as having descended from people here for centuries or millennia. The Know Nothings favored the same conflation, dressing as Native Americans to deride the Irish. You could see a similar alignment at taverns in the West post-9/11 when Confederate flags shared wall space with T-shirts showing Indigenous men on horses with the caption "Homeland Security: Fighting Terrorism since 1492." Populist anti-government and anti-immigrant sentiments can cross political divides in baffling ways.

At Mountain Meadows in southern Utah in 1857, white Mormon militiamen dressed in feather headdresses killed more than 120 non-Mormon wagon train travelers as they passed through remote country. Historians attribute the crime to "war hysteria" and fear of a federal invasion—the Mormons had been sparring with the feds over polygamy for decades—but also Mormon teachings of the era which denounced outsiders. Historians also note that initially the attackers intended to arm Northern Paiute men to commit the murders and that some of them did join the perpetrators, as if this fact justifies the costumes.

One day I sat talking about the dress-up phenomenon with Chris La Tray, a friend who is a member of the Little Shell Chippewa Tribe.

"It was such a cowardly move," I said. "A way to avoid being caught or to affix blame elsewhere, but also a kind of freedom, don't you think? An excuse to go crazy."

Chris nodded, unsurprised. "Right. They want to be *savages*. Now those same dudes go wild at football games."

In a story thick with parallels to contemporary times, I hadn't thought of this one. There are more than two thousand teams named for Indigenous people in the United States (including Braves, Chiefs, Indians, Orangemen, Raiders, Redmen, Reds, Redskins, Savages, Squaws, Tribe and Warriors, as well as tribe names such as Apaches, Arapahoe, Aztecs, Cherokees, Chickasaws, Chinooks, Chippewas, Choctaws, Comanches, Eskimos, Mohawks, Mohicans, Seminoles, Sioux and Utes). At games, with faces painted, white fans hoot and holler, wield oversized stuffed tomahawks. Even when Indigenous people beg them to stop, Chris said, they do not stop.

Over time I came to realize that people who considered the Chelan Falls Massacre tended to determine the culprits less on the meager facts than on the circumstances of their own political moment. Just as early settlers eagerly blamed Native people, many contemporary westerners I talked with were quick to latch onto the whites-as-attackers theory. I was no exception. On TV, white nationalists marched on Charlottesville chanting "We will not be replaced," and while mainstream podcasts argued whether the message on the Statue of Liberty was really meant to welcome refugees, the US government was separating children from their parents at the Mexican border. For two years, fury pervaded my social circles. Friends headed to El Paso to protest. Vanessa Gutierrez and the lawyers at the Northwest Immigrant Rights Project continued to be swamped. Xenophobia felt omnipresent and insidious. White racists seemed plenty capable of committing an atrocity and blaming non-whites.

Massacre aside, the historical parallels from that era and our own became alarming. The Chinese Exclusion Act of 1882, for example, proved to be less a blip than a blueprint. Immigration laws passed by the Trump administration rode those long coattails. A short list of immigration laws initiated or changed included undermining asylum, banning people from majority Muslim countries, reducing refugee acceptance, denying and delaying foreign worker requests (even though Trump had foreign workers in his own businesses), targeting pregnant women for exclusion, slowing applications for green cards and citizenship, attacking DACA, and going after naturalized citizens. Like Kearney, Trump cloaked oppression in name-calling—"animals," "rapists," from "shithole countries"—and justified every action with the same tiresome excuse: they're taking our work.

Often I thought about ditches.

Ditches, or remnants of them, run across dry hillsides near Chelan Falls, over ground so rocky you'd have to use explosives to maintain grade, and over gullies and creeks, propped by scaffolding. Chinese miners built the ditches to draw water from side creeks down to the main river, the Columbia, to run through sluice boxes and rinse out gold dust. Later, when the Chinese left, white settlers took them over for irrigation. They planted trees and watered them, started businesses and stayed.

At a wide spot along the highway, a historical marker tells the story of one such ditch. China Ditch, it's called. The sign is hard to see if you're not looking, and if you park on the shoulder and stand in the wind, even then you find it hard to see the ditch itself. Once you do, you see it's wider than you'd expect, more like a canal, hand dug. If you've done any digging in your life at all, you will know: this took a ton of work.

Sometimes when I think of how we landed here—me and Laurie, our seasonal friends, fourth-generation families, orchardists in Chelan, all of us—I picture those ditches. It's as though we're floating down a ditch of clear clean water. The cliché analogy for what I'm trying to describe is "having the wind at your back," and yeah, I know the feeling. I ride a bike enough to know how humiliating it is when you think you're so strong— you've been riding fast, making good time—and you turn to face the wind. No matter how many times it's happened. Even if you know which way the wind blows—downvalley day after day—it's still a shock. You had no idea how much help you had.

But here's the thing: no one worked like hell to build the wind.

Chapter Nine
UP THE LADDER

In the early morning in the hills above Chelan, I sat in my car sipping hot coffee from a thermos lid. Sets of headlights shone eerily in the predawn dark. Cars idled in rows between apple trees, one per row, as though each had its own assigned space, while drivers waited for the word: to work or not to work. I'd driven a steep winding road from pavement to dirt, past unmarked junctions into unlighted orchards, following a short line of cars and the printed directions in my lap to the place where I now sat with my coffee, studying the cheat sheet I'd scribbled of Spanish vocabulary words—*huerta, manzana, trabajar*—smelling rain-wet sage, watching the steady drizzle grow steadier, nervous and determined, waiting.

I'd hatched the plan in late summer, standing with a glass of chardonnay, a generous pour, on the deck of a local winery while gold-washed sun seeped into the vineyards. Friends had invited me to a fundraiser for Northwest Immigrant Rights Project (NWIRP), an over-busy organization these days. The regional office opened less than a decade ago with only two staffers, a lawyer and a clerk, and now they have a dozen lawyers and more work than they can handle. The crowd of milling donors was entirely white and older than me, the staff and attorneys non-white, female, and younger, the setting equal parts elegant—wine and appetizers, heels and sports coats—and rustic. Just inside the patio doors, rough pine siding sported taxidermy animals on every wall. Two cougars stalked the mantelpiece, lithe and fierce; a bull elk and an albino deer supervised the kitchen; and a single black bear stood coyly behind the podium with one arm raised, looking askance.

When the featured speaker stood in front of the bear to offer remarks, he pulled a slip of notebook paper from his back pocket. Luis Soto Benitez wore boots and jeans. He had a clean long-sleeved shirt, a work shirt, a working body, and an easy smile. He told his story plainly: how he emigrated from El Salvador when he was four years old, finished school, got married, and had a baby. When his job required him to get a commercial driver's license, his undocumented status was flagged, and he had to turn to NWIRP for help getting a green card. He was grateful, he said, and he smiled and sat. By the time he did, I'd made up my mind.

For months, I'd been stalled telling myself the problem with obsessing over Chinese miners was there's no way to find out what their lives were really like. But that's not all that had been bothering me. This was: there are plenty of people who live in the same time and place as me, more or less, who might as well dwell in another dimension. If I wanted to know more about people like Luis, I needed to shed the chardonnay and get to work. I left the event determined to find a job picking apples.

If it seemed a little cockamamie, a white middle-aged woman hauling a fifty-pound sack up and down ladders, orchardists seemed happy enough to consider the idea. They'd done their time, after all. They'd started as back-to-the-landers who arrived in the seventies, planting trees in spring, picking apples in fall, or they'd grown up on orchards, picking as a chore, near punishment. And to be clear, I'd picked apples, too, in Stehekin, but since that is not a commercial orchard, people like me can pick as much or as little as we'd like.

At any rate, the orchardists didn't seem to think it would be impossible for me to pick physically. But legally? That would be a challenge. Many family operations rely on the federal H-2A program, which allows them to employ seasonal guest workers from other countries so long as they house them adequately and pay their transportation to and from the US. The program requires a boatload of paperwork on any potential employee. To make the process worthwhile, you'd have to commit to the entire season, five or six weeks. Me, I hoped to survive half a week. So, they wished me luck and texted me a quote from Woody Guthrie. "You, too, can be a bum, a tramp, or an apple knocker."

Eventually friends of friends agreed to take me on. Over email, Monica Libbey was matter-of-fact, friendly, slightly bemused. Sure, she said, you can pick as much as you want. I packed for a week, settled on a friend's couch, prepared a huge lunch, woke at dawn, and drove in drizzle twenty-five miles to the worksite where now, one by one, sets of headlights emerged from the trees and pointed back down the hill.

Monica knocked on my window, smiling under a rain jacket hood: "We don't pick in the rain," she said. "I mean, we would if we were desperate, but we're not. Welcome to farming."

I'd signed up to pick for a week and the ferry to Stehekin runs only once a day—no chance to sneak home—so I was on my own in Chelan with no particular agenda.

Without my usual mile-long to-do list, town looked different. A few late-season tourists still window-shopped the brick storefronts for kitchen gadgets or beach accessories, but most businesses downtown—the espresso shop, the health food store, Kelly's Ace Hardware, Riverwalk Books—catered to locals or second-home owners. Nearly every vehicle on the street, from Subarus to Dodge Rams, had all-wheel drive. Nearly everyone was white.

At Walmart, just up the road past the high school football

field and the Les Schwab tire shop, it was all two-wheel-drive sedans, a decade older than the downtown rigs, not decrepit but not shiny either. Inside, most everyone—clerk and customer alike—was Latino. Several midday shoppers were young men. Two of them ahead of me in line held infant-sized onesies up to the clerk to ask about sizes. These must be my fellow pickers, I thought, these smooth-faced strong-backed boys, or barely-not boys, in super-clean white tennis shoes and trucker caps with wide flat brims.

If my presumption was grounded in bias, and God knows it was, it did have some basis in fact. While the list of eligible countries for H-2A includes ones from every continent except Antarctica, the lion's share of guest workers come from Mexico. But like the Chinese before them, they're not all guests. The 2010 census listed a quarter of Chelan County residents as Latino (and an even higher percentage in three surrounding rural counties—Adams, Grant, and Douglas) and many, but not all, of them do manual labor. According to one report from the Federal Small Business Administration, in 2012 about 4 percent of local businesses were Latino-owned, and more presumably are today. The whole saga is familiar, a slow assimilation, the way it worked for my immigrant grandparents: Come, work, stay! Move from making things to making money, and voila, you're a pillar of the community. That's how it's supposed to work.

On the third morning, the skies finally cleared and the orchard came to life. The trees stood no taller than ten or twelve feet high in uniform straight rows, a green wall of foliage more like broadly spaced cornstalks, in some ways, than classic picture-book trees. I'd parked in a treeless space with a small tractor and stacks of apple bins. At four by four feet wide and three feet deep, each bin could hold one thousand pounds of apples.

Monica greeted me and explained the routine. Pickers

would each work their own row. They'd be paid twenty-two dollars per bin and fill around ten bins a day—ten thousand pounds of apples each—and I was welcome to pick my own row, but, well... She smiled. We both knew I'd barely fill one bin. Or I could take turns working with each of the five other employees.

"I don't know if you want to talk," she said, "or if it's a head trip kind of thing."

"Both," I said, laughing.

And so it was decided: I'd pick and donate my apples to them. She introduced me to Juan, who checked the bins and served as a foreman of sorts—though he'd hate the label, I could already tell—and who would introduce me to the others.

One thing became immediately clear: these were not the white-shoed boys from Walmart. They wore soft boots and work pants, and they were older than I expected, much older. They also spoke Spanish almost exclusively, though this didn't surprise me. I came prepared to speak Spanish or at least to try. I learned as a kid because my mom was a Spanish teacher, and I learned again in high school and college classes, too many to count. Still, I could barely converse at the top of my game, and it had been twenty years since then, and nearly as long since I did physical labor all day.

By 7:05 I stood on a ladder with a bag over my shoulders, ready to pick. Piscar. Juan explained the basics. You wear the bag on your front. Set the fruit in the bag gently, never drop it. No bruising ever. Golpe. The first new word of the day. No golpes. And you never ever break off the stem. You hold it with one finger, while you twist upwards to remove the apple, stem and all. By the end of the day, my blistered index finger would be among my sorest body parts. Next new word: tupa. You must keep the tupa, he said. I picked ten apples before I lost my first stem. I held the apple up to Juan and lifted my eyebrow. Toss it? No, no. He motioned for me to put it in my bag and just keep moving. I picked. I watched. I picked.

The men picked fast, super fast, two hands moving in tandem, and filled the bags on their bellies in minutes. Then everything slowed. They laid the bag into a bin softly as laying a baby on a blanket, before they loosened the ropes to open the bag. The apples slid out, or more precisely, the bag slid from under the fruit, as the men reached across and cradled the apples as they came free, so they wouldn't roll and bruise. It was like a caress, and it was over fast, as they hustled back to their ladders, some at a half-jog.

The apples were large, weighty as a baseball, sometimes a softball, with stems thick as cord. The bins filled fast. José Luis, with whom I was paired first, had a system. He wanted the apples kept level as the bin filled, so when we emptied a bag, they wouldn't tumble into a low spot. Level, he showed me, patting his hands on air across an imaginary plain. Plano. I nodded. He smiled. I picked some more. We began to talk.

José Luis was forty-eight and a grandfather. He wore safety goggles and a Gilligan-style bucket hat, and he was the most careful and methodical of the pickers. When he moved his aluminum ladder, he shook it hard and jumped on the bottom rung before climbing, and he motioned to me to do the same. His wife worked at the Lake Chelan Clinic, he told me, and his kids, a son and a daughter, worked for the sheriff's department and a local veterinarian respectively. He came from Mexico in 2000, eighteen years ago, to find work—none to be had at home—and he'd stayed in the area since. Has he ever returned to Mexico? I asked. Have his kids? No, no, there's too much violence, he said. Much worse than when he left. He paused to climb down his ladder, bend into the bin, and empty his sack. When he stood upright, he readjusted his hat, and repeated his story once more for emphasis: he came because there was no work, but he stayed because of the violence.

I nodded. I picked. I watched. I picked. I listened.

I didn't come to do interviews, exactly. I came to work

because working is the best way I know to learn about anything or anyone, to talk easily, to feel the rhythm of a day, and with José Luis, I felt it. Music played in the distance, and a tractor engine growled as Juan drove around picking up full bins. José Luis complained about the ruido, said he prefers silence, but continued to chat amiably.

Blue sky filtered through leaves turning autumn yellow. Red windfall apples dotted the ground between the trees. Juan warned me not to trip on them, but I tripped anyway. I fell hard, bag and all, but recovered, apples and all. José Luis asked if I was okay. He told me his brother fell from a ladder and lost use of his hand permanently. Esta bien? Esta bien. Ten cuidado. All the while his two hands moved fast but not frantic, fluid as a drummer keeping a beat, a weaver making a rug. He filled his bag and emptied it, filled his bag and emptied it.

Every so often, Juan came round to check the bins, carrying tickets with the names of the employees and the name of the orchard. He tacked them to the bins with a staple gun. He handled the apples, moved them around. What are you checking for? I asked. He shrugged. Nothing right now. He also watched me unload. No golpes, I said. Meaning: I know. Meaning: I'm trying. He smiled, picked up my ladder, and gestured for me to follow him across the orchard. Time to rotate.

Music blared from a two-foot-high standalone speaker playing Pandora and running off a cord connected to a car's cigarette lighter. The female singers sounded like contestants on *The Voice*, quavering high notes and promises of amor, amor, amor. I couldn't tell if the huge speaker belonged to Antonio or Miguel. They worked in adjoining rows and took turns singing snips of love song lyrics in falsetto, all boy bluster and sniggers from men in their forties. Antonio, handsome, distractingly so, worked hatless in a blue plaid shirt. His bin was not plano like José Luis's. He was not as meticulous, but he was faster, maybe the fastest of them all, and as I tried to pick with him, for him, he met my stock questions with stock replies. He's from Mexico, yes, yes, been here twenty years. His wife works at an apple-packing shed. He has two kids. Does he like music? Sí, como no? His tone implied: Well, duh.

You? He asked. Married?

Suddenly I felt self-conscious, exposed.

No. Sola.

Why on earth did I lie? I was already an outsider. I wanted to fit in as much as possible, to find common ground. Only much later did I consider that showing my cards—owning up to the way I don't fit in—might have made me fit in better. At the time, I tried to concentrate on the task at hand, picking fast, trying and failing to keep up.

From the next row over, Miguel belted out another lyric: amor amor amor. He wore a bandanna under his ball cap to protect from the late-season gnats I'd expected and was glad not to find. Whatever its purpose, the bandanna gave him a festive and furtive air. He drank Monster energy drinks in tallboy cans and sometimes danced with his ladder. All the while, the bins filled. Juan's staple gun slapped over and over. Twenty-two dollars. A thousand pounds. Over and over.

The idea of unskilled labor is, of course, nonsense. What you need to know to be able to pick apples for a day compared to what you need to know to pick for a living is like what you need to write a sentence versus writing a novel. When I worked on trails, weekend volunteers appeared often, cocky and useless, certain they knew how to use a shovel or an axe—who doesn't?—when they didn't. There's slim space between romanticizing manual labor and condescending to people who would rather be doing anything else. Even dinner-prayer gratitude for the people who grow our food seems both earnest and treacherous. Are we glad they grew it or glad we didn't have to?

*

After lunch the music switched to ranchera—male voices, accordions, a polka beat—and Antonio did not dig it. He liked the other kind better, but they must've had an arrangement, he and Miguel, a truce, because Miguel loved the ranchera, clearly, and once I was working with him, he answered my questions curtly, in English insistently, and bantered with Antonio over my head. When Pandora died, he pulled up his car, opened the doors, and turned on the radio—more ranchera music—even louder. Maybe to annoy Antonio. Maybe to keep from talking to me. But at this point, I was not chatty. The muscles between my shoulder blades had knotted hard, predictably, and less predictably, bruises had formed on my shins from bracing hard against ladder rungs while picking with two hands. No use trying to banter. I wasn't a real worker, so the banter was not real, and Miguel, in his way, was calling my bluff. Turns out I'm no Studs Terkel. I don't even like that book. I just wanted to work.

And even when I was in pain this seemed like good work to me—outdoors, independent, physical, better than a cubicle any day—and if you can work your way up to picking ten bins, $220 for an eight-hour day is not a bad wage. But I'd never fit in doing it for real. We live in work bubbles. You often hear Sunday is the most segregated day of the week, but here it was a Wednesday and there were no white people to be found, not on this orchard or from what I could tell, on any of the surrounding ones, and very few women. These men had staked a place for themselves, and the question I skirted around all day was this: Did their place, their work, their livelihood, or God forbid their lives, feel threatened? They were working legally, make no mistake, but beyond that, the specifics of their situations were lost to language and common courtesy, or some level of fear. Not too different, I imagine, from why I didn't talk about my wife.

With an hour left to work, I tucked my ladder under one arm, ducked under limbs, and went to find my last picking partner, another José. He was younger by fifteen years than the other men, and he'd only been at this orchard for ten days, not twenty years—pickup labor, not part of the regular crew; he shows up and waits at the beginning of each harvest: cherries, peaches, apples—and he had a cold bottle of water and a can of Pepsi for me from the communal cooler waiting by his bin, a gesture kind enough to reset my mood. My tongue had loosened, nerves abated from exhaustion, Spanish synapses firing at last, and José was eager to tell his story. He grew up in Mexico, in Guerrero, near the ocean; he had a boat and loved to fish. He met his wife there when they were both fourteen, and when they crossed the border together as brand-new adults, it was difficult, but worth it. He wasn't talking about escaping violence, not talking about finding work either; he was beaming, talking about moving on, discovering new places. Like Chicago, a city he loves, a beautiful city, a city full of life, where they lived for a while before moving again to nearby Bridgeport, an hour from here, upriver on the Columbia. Would he like to do another kind of work? I asked. Claro que sí. Sure, but for now there was always fruit to be picked. He had two kids, eight and thirteen, and he coached their futbol teams. They loved sports like he loved sports, and he wanted them to experience fishing the way he knew fishing, so last Christmas they went to Mexico and the kids loved it. Did he worry about violence? Sure, but the fishing was tremendous. The other men seemed settled, accustomed to things, realistic and resigned. But for José, anything could happen still. When Juan called quitting time, José didn't quit. He stayed at it as long as he could, trying to get a few more apples in the bin.

In 2012, when the study of Latino-owned businesses was published, things were looking up. If there could be less political pressure on would-be Latino customers, the authors concluded, less omnipresent fear of deportation, real or perceived, and less prejudice from would-be non-Latino customers, too, existing businesses would thrive and more would start. The researchers wrote as if those "if"s were really "when"s. But that was 2012, this was 2018. Things had soured—and could sour worse—in a thousand different ways: the stroke of a pen, an overzealous sheriff, citizens, local or otherwise, turned bitter and reactionary. I tried to picture these men and their families decades in the future. If things went well, their kids would become part of the fabric of the country, searchable someday in the local historical museum, their rights having been heroically protected by the young lawyers at the winery. But if things got worse, it was hard for me to imagine any of these men turning to the good people at Northwest Immigrant Rights Project for help, desperation no match for their pride.

If things got tough enough, I figured they'd just move on.

Chapter Ten
DOWSING

Dorothy Petry walked with a cane over rough plank floors from one room to the next at the Depot Museum in Oroville—thirty miles west of Chesaw—narrating as she went. She traced the routes the Northern Pacific Railroad took when it came through the region in 1906 and explained a map of the customs houses along Lake Osoyoos. Her thin gray hair cut no-nonsense short, she wore spectacles and a white school-teacher cardigan, but exuded more enthusiasm than authority, more sly humor than stodginess. She stopped near a display about Hiram Smith, an early white settler in the region who's sometimes called "Okanogan Smith." She tapped his portrait, leaned forward, and told me how, after a fruitless search of several years, she found his gravesite. Which boded well for our mission. She'd invited me along to find Chee Saw's grave.

Actually, I invited myself. I wanted to see Chesaw in spring and to visit again with Arnie Marchand, the amiable docent I'd met at the Depot Museum who'd told me his ancestors killed more than seven hundred Chinese people near Chelan Falls. I figured he had to have been exaggerating or pulling my leg. Randy Lewis had been adamant: white men murdered the miners. If Arnie Marchand was going to claim his people committed the massacre and, in fact, killed off twice as many people as anyone else dared admit, well, I had to give him a chance to renege.

Back when I first met him, Arnie had brushed off my questions about the Chinese. He clearly found them uninteresting, or worse, distracting, a side story, a minor subplot, in the centuries-long history of his people. But he told me about Dorothy, his "eighty-year-old friend" who could answer my questions.

"She loves this stuff," he'd said.

I waved him off, still thinking this was just a side trip on a side trip on my massacre research, but once I was home I wrote him an email saying I liked his book *The Way I Heard It* and asked about his friend.

By spring I had a regular pen pal. Dorothy Petry kept keen notes and followed obscure threads. She'd already chased down enough information about Hiram Smith to piece together a full biography. I wasn't interested in Smith. My impatience with white settler history bordered on derision. White men wreaked havoc on the frontier—we know this—and yet, still, small historical societies all over the rural West often glorify them to the exclusion of others—women, immigrants, Indigenous people especially. For all my searching I'd yet to meet anyone descended from Chee Saw despite having climbed out on twiggy limbs of the family tree, sending countless emails to strangers on both sides of the border. But Dorothy Petry and her fellow historical society volunteers, Mike and Kay Sibley, claimed Chee Saw as their own. They revered him as an original settler, a person of stature. If they wanted to find his grave, I was all in.

Dorothy went to work negotiating a visit to Chee Saw's former property along Myers Creek. The place is not hard to pinpoint. A 1934 map indicates which plat belonged to Chee Saw's daughter, "Julia Chesaw" (though in most other documents she uses her mother's surname, "Lum") and also notes that it had originally been an allotment. Dorothy knew that a new owner had recently bought the place, and to get there we'd have to cross another property, so she planned to assemble three different sets of stakeholders: the former property owner, the new ones, and the owner of the property we'd cross. She'd tried before with no success. Now she was determined. I'd made a plan to meet with Arnie Marchand on Tuesday, and the grave search got scheduled, by happenstance, on Monday. Dorothy kept me abreast of the plans, and only after weeks of correspondence did she slip in a new phrase.

Dowsing, she wrote. We'd be going grave dowsing.

I had no idea what she meant, but it was too late to back out.

In Oroville, Dorothy, her daughter, Ellen, and I grabbed lunch at the America Café because every other restaurant in town was closed on Monday. Ellen, in blue jeans and a T-shirt, her long hair streaked with gray, helped her mother slide into the booth, and just as we ordered food, Arnie Marchand walked in.

He did not say hello. He did not make eye contact. He sat in the booth directly behind us with two other men, either brothers or cousins, Dorothy thought, and when I craned my neck to say hello, he ignored me. I could guess why. I'd traveled to Oroville ostensibly to see him, and now I was sitting with Dorothy feeling middle-school awkward. Only the situation was rifer than that. We sat in a café called "America" after all, and I'd come in search of answers not just about Chee Saw but about race and exclusion, too, and now I was sitting in a small-town café segregated by race, thinking of how we do and don't talk to one another.

After lunch, Mike and Kay Sibley pulled up in a fourteen-passenger van. The middle-aged couple greeted me warmly and Dorothy even more warmly, like family, their attitudes bemused and deferential at once. Both of them, I'd learn, were former teachers and lifelong residents of the region. Kay, the executive director of the Borderlands Historical Society, carried a slight air of authority. Mike, the only man in the group, had a shrugging just-along-for-the-ride cheerfulness. We climbed in and set off on a lark, an adventure, a springtime drive.

"Let's do this," Kay said, unrolling a couple of plat maps.

Turned out no one was clear on Chee Saw's trajectory in

the area. One local historian, the late Ruth Wiltz, claimed in a newspaper article from the 1990s to have a document from a US. Indian agent claiming Chee Saw lived in a "tee pee" on his wife's allotment until he was kicked off. The article quoted Wiltz saying the agency "decided the land had too much value so they threw it out to the homesteaders and wouldn't allow him to live on it." Dorothy would later loan me a thumb drive of photographed handwritten pages from the office of the same Indian agent to look for evidence, and the handwriting would prove so horrible I'd have to hire a student with better eyesight to go through them, one by one. No dice. The student found no evidence of eviction.

Meanwhile, in the van, we checked out a couple spots where Chee Saw may have spent time before landing at Myers Creek, but no one was certain which were legit.

They did, however, know for certain where Hiram Smith lived. We stopped to see his modest cabin—weathered pine logs canted square with moss sticking out of the ancient chinking— and an apple tree Smith planted, too, a very old tree, a survivor, an unknown variety with gnarled bark and unpruned limbs. I ran my fingers over the bark and examined the small fruit rotting on the ground left behind by birds and bears—the apples weren't sweet enough, apparently, for humans to bother—and climbed back into the van to continue on.

We followed a gravel road along an old railroad grade. The Great Northern went back and forth across the border, Dorothy explained, a thriving route finished in 1906 and later abandoned. We noted a few more possible places where Chee Saw may have lived. Maybe by the dilapidated barn? Maybe farther down the draw? We watched the green hillsides, the mountaintops newly snow-free, the sky a mottled white, and suddenly someone noticed a plume of smoke on the horizon, a too-early wildfire, only mid-May.

"Where is it?" I asked.

Kay shrugged. "Maybe in Canada," she said.

"Is the border close?" I asked.

"It's right there," Kay said with a chuckle.

Turned out, despite my struggles to find the exact line last time I visited, the border sat in plain sight, a barbed wire fence in wide open country. You could duck under and walk for miles, just as I'd suspected.

"Could I hop right over?" I asked.

"No way."

No single crossing goes undetected, my hosts explained. Cameras monitor every inch of the fence, and if you cross alarms go off everywhere—in border patrol offices and vehicles, over handheld radios. Just as I suspected. Ellen told a story about friends who'd gone hunting, with maybe five weapons, and crossed the border by accident because the road they'd driven north had thawed to deep impassable muck. Boy, were they in trouble. Guns are serious business in Canada, she said. Crossing the border is serious, too, unless you're preapproved. The four passengers in the van with me all had enhanced driver's licenses so they could breeze across anytime, for Chinese food in Osoyoos, say, and be back in an hour.

"What about the Chinese in Chee Saw's time?" I asked. "You think it was easy for them?"

"No way," Kay said, emphatic now. "It was just like the Mexicans now. They were targets."

Dorothy remained silent.

When you reach the town of Chesaw, the Mercantile is the first building you pass. Two stories tall with a gravel parking lot, the place sells a mishmash of staples and sundries: saltine crackers, postcards, canned goods. We entered and passed a chest freezer near the door, from which Mike and Kay and Dorothy each selected an ice cream. They sat down casually with two women in tie-dyed shirts in their sixties at a round table in the middle of the store.

Since it looked like we were settling in for a while, I decided to buy an ice cream for myself. In front of me, a young man and woman, bedraggled hippie types, stood at the register with four bags of ice. We waited at the register for several minutes—the ice bags dripping, my ice-cream bar melting—before I slowly realized the two women at the table must be the proprietors, and they were in no hurry to take our money.

If this were Chee Saw's store, I wondered, would he do the same? Eye the clientele, gauging them while they silently waited, or find easy humor by testing their patience? In my mind, his store would be orderly, well-stocked. He was a seasoned merchant, looking to make real money, and the town itself was on the upswing, a place to get ahead, not a place to hide. But how could I know? Ignorance obscured the past like road dust on a rear window. Maybe Chesaw was as forgotten then as now. Maybe Chee Saw was weary. Maybe his wife ran the show. Some histories called his wife Susan Seymour, but Dorothy corrected me in the van.

"Not Seymour, LUM," she said. "Susan LUM."

Maybe Chee Saw smoked a pipe, legs outstretched, feet crossed, listening to conversations skirt trouble.

So too with the tie-dye proprietors and my hosts. Extremes flourish out here: gun rights and property rights, strict religion and lax drug enforcement. Best not to mouth off. Even with these motley grave hunters, I had to watch myself. I'd noticed Ellen saying silent grace over her salad at the America Café and later learned she's married to a Yakama man, and together they sawed, split, and stacked firewood for cash. And while Kay and Mike had lived their whole lives in the Okanogan, they were hardly parochial. Kay, who was born on an apple orchard and taught home economics before settling into a job as the school librarian, told me she traveled all over the world each year to backpack with her daughter. Stereotypes carried no more weight in Chesaw than a time schedule. Which is to say: none at all.

At last the owners of the property where we thought Chee Saw once lived—all three sets—began to arrive.

First came the man whose land we'd have to cross. He'd given us permission, but he did not plan to join us and made no small talk, except to discuss the soft earth, newly plowed, and whether these city rigs could make it across. Next up: Dale Duchow who very recently purchased the land where Chee Saw's house once stood. Dale sported a gray Kenny Rogers–style beard and radiated cheer either exaggerated or strained. He brought his wife, also in her sixties, and while they both acted game for this grave hunt, Dale especially remained transparently skeptical.

Last came Chris Colbert, whose family owned the land for a long time before Dale bought it. I asked him to repeat his last name into the digital recorder I'd brought along.

"Coal-Burt," he said. He did not want his name pronounced like the television comedian, Stephen Colbert. "I hate that guy," he said.

He reached out a hand to shake mine. He was a trim man in Levi's, a flannel shirt, and an oil-stained ball cap advertising Napa Auto Parts. He was polite and watchful, not likely to miss a thing.

We transferred from the van to four-wheel-drive pickups to cross the new-plowed field, passed a single horse grazing, and stopped at a barbed wire fence overlooking Myers Creek. We climbed through one at a time, with Dorothy coming last with her cane and her white pants and tennies and help from Ellen. She ducked through the wires, stood straight in the wind, grinning wide, and turned three sixty to take in the view.

Below us, Myers Creek ran shallow and narrow, shaded by willows and brambles, and on the far side the main highway ran east toward the cemetery. At one time, Chris explained, a horse ford crossed right there. We could see where the old trail grade split the gentle slope below where we stood. Dorothy followed his arm gesturing outward and nodded in agreement.

Right here. This was where Chee Saw's cabin once stood. He may or may not have had a store—most accounts only say he gardened and sold the vegetables—but his home was definitely along this trail just above the horse ford where he would have interacted with nearly everyone passing through.

Dorothy tucked herself in, out of the wind, turned her back toward the crowd, and reached into her cardigan pocket. She pulled out a white crystal the size of the tip of my index finger attached to a lightweight gold chain. She caught my eye and grinned mischievously.

"Dowsing," she said. "This will tell us where the grave is."

I tried not to react, to show any surprise or disappointment, tried to mimic the respect Mike and Kay modeled, gentle solemnity, genuine anticipation.

Dale, not so much.

"Are you saying you can find dead bodies with a crystal?" he asked.

"Yes, yes. Okanogan Smith's body was missing for 118 years, and I found it," Dorothy replied.

"Can you find gold mines, too?"

"I have not tried gold mines."

At this point, Mike and Kay weighed in, admitting they hadn't been believers at first—the first indication I had that they'd known about the crystal in advance—but when Dorothy accurately dowsed their septic drainfield, they were converted. I considered their credulity. Truth is, I'd had a similar experience years earlier when a retired Chelan orchardist and self-described "Arkie" successfully dowsed our well in Stehekin using one-year-old applewood. When he stood at the place where he said two underground rivers converged, the applewood trembled and bent. We had well drillers aim for that spot, saved a ton of money, and have had excellent water for twenty years since. I'd even had the dowser teach me to do it myself. I couldn't make applewood bend, but with two bent coat hangers I could find underground pipes or an electrical line, no problem. Still, I thought, it's a long way from water under the surface to century-old bones.

I held my tongue.

Dorothy stood in knee-high weeds in the shadows of snow-patched hills, three miles from the border, surrounded by spectators, and asked the crystal quietly whether it would be okay to ask some questions. If the crystal sways front to back, she explained, the answer is yes. If the crystal sways side to side, the answer is no.

The answer was yes, and so she began.

Are the graves to my right between me and the creek? YES
Are the people buried down there all Chinese? NO
Is the man known as Chee Saw buried there? YES

"Is this like a Ouija board?" Dale intruded, smirking again, smirking still.

"No. I will not use a Ouija board. I can make a Ouija board talk. Believe me, I could make a Ouija board talk until I found out a Ouija board is not good. I believe the power of witching actually comes from a different source."

"And nobody has burned you at the stake yet?"

"Not yet."

Chris Colbert stood on the outside of the circle we'd formed. He remained an observer, reserving comment, except as questions of geography arose, then he jumped in. His people came west from Benton County, Missouri, he explained, and they owned this parcel of land, Chee Saw's land, for more than eighty years.

"When I used to farm this with my horses, I'd find bones all the time because the Indians used to camp here because, it's funny, the wind can be blowing thirty-five here and you go down there and it's calm. No wind at all. The trail came up and there was the ford, so they camped at that meadow."

Dorothy listened, nodded, glad for Chris's precision and camaraderie, then she dove in again.

> Was he buried there before 1900? YES
> Was he buried there after 1895? YES
> Was he buried there in 1897? NO
> Was he buried there in 1898? YES

These answers sounded about right, or at least in the ball-park. According to another amateur historian, Lucille McDonald, "When Chee Saw's wife died, he is reported to have moved to Alberta and married a Chinese woman. In the 1920s, it is understood, he returned to China to die. Another report has it that he died in Okanogan County in 1897." Or 1898?

> Is Chee Saw's wife Susan buried near him? YES
> Are any of Chee Saw and Susan's children buried down there? NO
> Do we have any Native Americans or First Nations people buried down there? YES

We'd been in the field a long while, but Dorothy showed no signs of wearying, and we stayed with her. She asked about the exact location of the house, tried to figure out where the door had been. At Dale's urging, she asked more about gold, but there was none, she said emphatically, or only a little, and he was disappointed, his interest having become abundantly clear. The questions came fast and furious, and the farther Dorothy strayed from asking strictly about the ground we stood on, the murkier the answers became. She asked how Chee Saw entered the country, through California (NO) or Canada (NO) whether he was considered a commoner in China (NO) or a merchant (NO) whether he died of natural causes (YES).

Chris spoke up. "I've never been able to dowse but I'm kinda gifted with a sixth sense especially with history and stuff. I'll tell you…you probably don't believe in reincarnation. I do."

"Well, I don't," Dorothy interrupted. "But that's okay."

"Anyway, my grandpa came here in 1906. I have pictures of him, and I look just like him, and there's stuff that I knew about horses and stuff I knew about this place and stuff I knew about Chee Saw that nobody ever told me."

"Oh, I believe in that too," Dorothy said. "I just call it intuition."

Ellen stepped in. "Intuition is what I would say. I don't believe in the reincarnation part but intuition. We totally believe in that."

Kay's cell phone rang, and she stepped aside to take the call, then tugged on my sleeve to get my attention. "It's Arnie Marchand," she said. "He wants to know if you have your papers."

"Papers?"

"To go to Canada," Kay said. "A passport?"

I told her I did, and she relayed the information and reported that Arnie would take me to Canada in the morning.

"He also wants me to tell you that if you thought he was rude in the café, you were right." Kay repeated the dig, more challenge than apology, not without humor. I was unfazed—I hadn't found him rude, more standoffish than anything—and, at any rate, I was glad to have a plan.

Energy waned. The sun stayed high only because of how far north we were a short month before summer solstice. If I wanted to get more information, now would be the time. I fed more questions to Dorothy, ones we'd pondered via email over the winter. Was Chee Saw known as Ah Chee? (NO) Did he have a store at Chelan Falls? (YES)

The answers felt neither definitive nor worth dismissing, deeply mystifying and oddly validating. Some spirit held the memory of these deaths, these years, these details, even if it was Dorothy's own faith or knowledge manifested. I could never make the leap Dorothy had to consider this source as reliable as—or more than—my file folders back home stuffed full of clippings with the kinds of carefully cited details Dorothy, as a pen pal, had been a stickler for. Dorothy straddled the worlds with ease, and I admired her for it. When backpacking alone, I've occasionally set up my tent and felt a presence, sometimes warm and right, sometimes menacing. I've moved camp for this reason more than once. At Myers Creek, I felt nothing so ethereal. I felt the easy camaraderie of these people, and that was enough for me. Dorothy headed to the place in the fence where Ellen held two strands of barbed wire wide apart so her mother could step back through.

On the long drive home, I thought of how strange the day had been, how close I'd felt to Chee Saw. Even though this was not written history, not oral history, it was, crystal aside, a kind of grounded history. To stand where he once stood, with others who cared that he had stood there, had moved me.

Chapter Eleven
FORGET JOHN WAYNE

At nine sharp, a red Buick tore into the parking lot at the only motel in town. Arnie Marchand beckoned me over impatiently through the driver's side window. I hurried to the passenger side, let myself in, and before I finished fastening my seatbelt he dove right in.

"I don't know what you want from me," he said, his tone all sly humor and straight talk.

He didn't wait for an answer. He explained the plan for the day instead. We'd aim north for Canada, he said, for a meeting he had scheduled with Clarence Louie, chief of the Osoyoos Band, one of eight Syilx communities, including the Federated Tribes of the Colville Reservation, that make up the Syilx Okanagan Nation, which straddles the international border. Otherwise he set aside the entire day for me.

"And I have no idea what you want to see."

No use beating around the bush. I explained my interest in the Chelan Falls massacre and reminded him he once told me that his people killed seven hundred Chinese men near Chelan Falls.

"Yes, yes." He swept one hand through the air, swatting this nonsense concern away, and doubling down at the same time, as if to say: *So what if we did.* That's not what he cared to talk about. He wanted to talk Indigenous history, take the long view. He had a captive audience, and he had a good point besides. Why bother with the Chinese people who came and went? Why not learn the story of the people who'd been here all along? He started at the beginning, or one of the beginnings, with David Thompson, the first white explorer to encounter the Syilx in 1781. "So he got his little canoes and he started down the river, and he pulled in at Kettle Falls and he met with them and this is the first white guys we ever saw, so the chief and David Thompson sat in the middle and all the men sat around there and all the women and children and the old people sat on the outside, so they had one of these guys get up and count all the men. Then he multiplied that by seven."

He meant there was no accurate count of the people he encountered—there could be none.

"Where did he come up with seven as a multiplier?"

"He's a white guy." Arnie gave me side-eye as he drew out the long *I* in white. "So, you never know. That's what he came up with. So he said there were four-hundred-some in that 'tribe.' And he went twenty more miles, found some people who lived down by Nespelem and there were almost an equal amount there, and he said they were another tribe, and then he got to Pateros and said they were the Methow tribe and then he passed two or three other little villages along the river and he came to another place called Entiat. Must be a tribe! Got to the mouth of Chelan and that was a tribe. Got to Wenatchee. Another tribe!"

They're all Syilx people, he meant. There was no real difference among them. Not then. Not now.

We drove north toward the border, past fruit orchards and summer homes along Lake Osoyoos, and Arnie stayed steadfastly in the early nineteenth century.

I tried to spur the timeline along. "Then in the 1870s trouble starts…"

"All anybody ever asks about is the 1880s, the 1890s. Just a few years. I call it the John Wayne period. That's not even history.

Just forget John Wayne." He sighed. "So Alexander Ross got here in 1811 and built Fort Okanagon out of sagebrush and driftwood."

"Then other white guys start coming in? Right away?"

"No."

"Jesuits?"

"No. They had a couple of them damned Catholics come through in 1834, but there weren't really any white people here. Caravan after caravan started coming through about 1840, but they hadn't even started coming yet. They hadn't crossed the Mississippi."

"So the Chinese came first?" Hell-bent I was to get back to the Chinese.

"No! Hiram Smith arrived in 1859. He was twenty-nine and married a fourteen-year-old, which was marrying age, and he paid through the nose for that Indian girl, and they put up a little place."

"And were your people starting to get worried?"

More side-eye. This time with a grimace.

"You gotta understand. Indians didn't get together and sit down and say boy, we're really worried about this. This had been happening all over Indian Country. We'd been hearing about this for two hundred years. Two hundred!"

We pulled up to the booth at the border. A Canadian official took Arnie's tribal membership card, which amounts to a kind of dual citizenship, and my passport, scanned them into a computer, and waved us through without small talk or delay. Arnie picked up where he left off. He took a few stabs at "greedy little Okanogan Smith," meant to undercut the reverence for the man on proud display at the Depot Museum. Then he cut to the chase.

"So gold was discovered up here, and those guys found a way to screw the Indians out of their land, and pretty soon they just took it over. From the Cascade Mountains to the Okanogan

River all the way to Chelan. From the border down. They just took it all."

By any measure, his succinct summation checks out. Displacement happened fast. In 1879, President Rutherford B. Hayes set up the so-called Moses Reservation to include the whole region exactly as Arnie described—from the Cascade crest to the Okanogan River, from Canada south to the Columbia. In 1887, the US Congress passed the Dawes Act to allow government officials to subdivide reservations and "allot" acreage to individual tribal members who could, in turn, sell the land for cash money. In 1888, gold discovered along Myers Creek—right where Chee Saw had settled, right where Dorothy dowsed graves the day before—brought swarms more white would-be settlers into the region who snapped up land the Native people sold cheap. In other words, in the course of a dozen years, the Syilx had their land stolen, then given back to them, then redistributed to them as individuals who promptly sold it back to the people who'd stolen it.

"Why'd they sell the allotments?"

"They were probably starving. They couldn't work anywhere. No one would hire them. They had to go somewhere. Cows were killing all the food, the medicine, all the berries. They've got no food left. They can't afford cows. So Tonasket and Moses come along…"

Arnie launched into a tirade against the best known "chiefs" of the era, Moses in the south, Tonasket in the north, both of whom negotiated extensively with the US government.

"You don't have much use for those guys," I said.

"They were just backstabbers, gold diggers. The white people thought a lot of them, though."

For a moment I considered how places are named, and for whom. If the nearby town of Tonasket was named for one backstabber and Moses Coulee was named for another, what does the name Chesaw say about Chee Saw? Maybe he wasn't so noble.

But what about the other Chinese people? The ones who went over the cliff.

"So where'd you get this seven hundred number? That they killed seven hundred Chinese miners?"

"That was just a guess because we killed them all over the place."

"When they started coming up here?"

"No, we killed them down there between Chelan and the Methow. We killed them all over the place."

I told him what Randy Lewis told me about how white men did the killing.

"They dressed up," I said.

Arnie shook his head in disgust. "No, no, no."

The clouds settled in the crooks of tree-thick mountains as we pulled into the parking lot of a large modern facility, low-profile, glass-fronted, consisting of interlocking circular structures rather than hard corners, the main offices and gathering space for the Osoyoos Indian Band. While Arnie met with the chief, I sat in a chair watching the mist turn to drizzle outside and reading up on the Osoyoos.

Clarence Louie has served as the chief since 1985 when he was twenty-four, and he's proved himself to be a wildly effective leader and businessman. The four hundred members of the Osoyoos Indian Band now own Nk'Mip Cellars, the first Native-owned winery in North America, one that employs twice as many people as there are band members. Still, it would take me a long while to figure out why Arnie Marchand brought me on this errand, which may or may not have been crucial, a question about granting access to tribal resources to some students from the US that could easily have been answered via email or over the phone. Either way, he didn't need to bring me along. Maybe it was kill-two-birds kind of day-planning. Or maybe it was a chance to show off. The Osoyoos story is a modern-era success story. Arnie is no chamber of commerce type, but he's not going to play the victim either. His long rambling stories were meant to showcase the widest possible swath of history, including the present. When we got back in the car, we visited the winery, the museum, all new, all impressive, made to order for the millions of tourists who visit this dry sunny corner of Canada each year, nearly a desert by that nation's standards. I told him Chelan attracts a lot of tourists for the same reason.

"Let me tell you this about Chelan. They were a six-month summer community. We got there, and they became a twelve-month, year-round vineyard winery nonstop tourist destination."

"Because of Mill Bay Casino?"

"Because of us! We are leading the charge!"

We crossed back over the border—American officials no more concerned with us or our documents than the Canadians had been—and continued south. He pointed out sites as we drove, where his ancestors lived along the river, in pit houses at first, as big as twenty feet around with a roof and an open fire in the middle. Later they switched to teepees or tule-mat-topped dwellings because they were easier to pack up and move.

"But anyway, we lived right down there until 1781 with the disease. I asked my aunt Louise this question. Tell me how you guys remade yourselves with so many gone. She said they did what you do when all the studs are gone, you go and get one. Went to Montana, went to Idaho. Brought them home."

"So there's a lot of different blood mixed in?"

"She said anybody who tells you they're full-blooded Okanagan is full of it. She said nobody's been a full blood around here since 1781. They could be full-blooded Indians, but not all Okanagan."

"Maybe that's why they weren't so worried about the Chinese coming in and marrying the Indians—because they needed men?"

"No. No we didn't."

"I read there's a whole bunch of Chinese blood."

"It's only in a couple of families."

I was frustrated by Arnie's resistance, as though even the possibility were an affront. Such pride in purity has always made me bristle. As the child of mixed European ancestry, the descendant of restless displaced, un-placed people, I feel judged, excluded, ashamed. I was quiet for a beat or two looking out the window at the fields and farmland and cloud-swathed hills, ready to let Arnie lead the conversation elsewhere for a while, but he chose to linger.

"You keep asking about the Chinamen. What do you want to know?"

"I told you what Randy Lewis said about the massacre, and you told me that was hogwash. And I asked you why those Chinese got killed, and you told me because they were everywhere and they were annoying."

"There were a lot of good reasons for not liking them."

"What are the other ones?"

"See this?" He pointed out an iron fence on the edge of Oroville stenciled with various images: an apple, a salmon. "I had the idea and got us some grant money, and over two years, the high school shop teacher did all that with his students."

"It's fantastic."

"Give a lazy guy a hard job and he'll find an easy way to do it." Arnie grinned wide.

I was getting used to the rhythm of the banter. Evade and confront. Ebb and flow. It was my turn.

"You still didn't tell me why they killed the Chinese."

"Well, I did. They were everywhere."

We stopped for a long lunch at a café, not the America, and ordered sandwiches and cold drinks, settled into small talk, then slowly more personal talk.

"My kids don't know anything about racism," he said out of the blue. "But I do."

He remembered being in the army in Texas in 1964 and not being served at a restaurant. He and his six buddies got up and left. They were in uniform. His kids don't know anything like that, he said. They can't even imagine it. Before the war? He was senior class president at Omak High School, thirty miles down the road, and he made a goal for himself: to ask thirteen girls out. All of them said yes, but each one came back after the weekend and said no. Their fathers wouldn't let them.

"They weren't about to let them date a damned Indian," he said.

He was skinny, too, a little guy. When he was younger in Omak, a guy beat him up, but his older brother took care of that. He had fourteen brothers and sisters.

"Used to be all we had around here was Indians."

But that changed. When World War II started, most of the boys left, and the girls went to work in the factories, and while they were gone, there was a shortage of laborers.

"This town hired 430 Mexicans to work the fruit. By the time I was getting out of high school, Indian kids stopped working in orchards. They stopped having two weeks off in the fall to harvest. They just stopped all that."

"Who is they?"

"The government! By the 1970s, you could count on one hand how many Indians were working in an orchard, generally they were old ones who couldn't do anything else. Now it's all Mexicans."

We were the only ones seated in the place, and the waitress had been waiting for a break to refill our iced tea. She filled them, and stepped away, and once more Arnie picked up his refrain.

"So I don't even know what you want to know."

"My whole deal is these Chinese, but it seems like it's not much of a thing from your perspective?"

"The Chinaman thing is nothing to me. It was such a little minor incident in our history. Compared to the Indians that lived here, it only lasted about three or four years. There's no way to look at it, no way to dive into it. Nobody wrote about it."

He was right, of course. That was the problem. If only a paper trail would miraculously appear, all of my questions would be answered. That's what happened a few hundred miles south, in the northeast corner of Oregon. There in 1887, in a cove along the Snake River in Hells Canyon, seven white men brutally murdered thirty-four Chinese miners. When the bodies—and body parts—washed up downriver, a local newspaper suggested the massacre amounted to a "severe warning to the Chinese miners." A year later, one man confessed, three were tried and found innocent. Later yet, Richard Harris, a Baker City businessman, offered a $10,000 reward for anyone who could prove or disprove the massacre occurred. For more than a century, nobody could.

Then, in 1995 a cache of documents showed up as a donation to the Wallowa County Museum—they'd not been lost so much as hidden—and Greg Nokes, a reporter for the *Oregonian* newspaper at the time, began to investigate the story. For his book *Massacred for Gold*, Nokes traced the history of the massacre back to the State Department, the correspondence of the Sam Yup Benevolent Association and some sloppy bragging by locals. His book spawned a bestselling novel, a poetry collection, and episodes of a TV show about ghosts in the area. In 2012, Nokes stood on the banks of the Snake River, near the site of the murders, in a remote roadless area of Hells Canyon, to see the dedication of a granite memorial to the murdered miners in three languages: Chinese, English, and Nez Perce.

We left the café and Arnie drove me back to the hotel to retrieve my own car and head back down the road. We could see, still, the wildfire I'd seen the day before burning on the horizon. I'd read in the newspaper it was in Canada, near Fraser Lake, and nearing 260 hectares.

"It's early, don't you think?" I asked.

"Well, it hasn't rained in forever. You could walk up that hill and kick up dust."

"Are you worried at all?"

"It comes every year," Arnie said, pausing for dramatic effect. "It's called summer."

Chapter Twelve
WHOSE HERITAGE?

Laurie and I walked hand-in-hand toward the square dance in a thick haze of smoke. The annual Stehekin event, sponsored by a nonprofit heritage foundation whose members help support the orchard, generates an old-timey vibe and awkward gender roles and loads of genuine affection. Raindrops, raisin-sized and far-between, spattered the cement foundation where everyone gathered. The foundation is all that's left of the original apple-packing shed, all that's been left for decades. The heritage foundation rebuilt it a few years back for community gatherings like this—it's level and largish, an ideal outdoor dance floor among the aging trees. The sky was a sickly orange brown, the mountains ghostly silhouettes. The raindrops weren't enough to do any good. A wildfire burned only ten miles away.

Not that anyone was too worried. We have fires every August. We suppressed them for too long, experts say, for a hundred years, but the forests need fire, so now they're burning hotter than ever. Plus there's climate change. One thing, though, that was different this time: the mountain between the fire and us burned already a few years back. There wasn't as much fuel as there once was, fewer leaves and needles, less underbrush. That didn't mean it wouldn't burn again, but it might not burn as hot.

The older crowd sat by the sidelines, spectating under Christmas lights rigged onto prop poles, powered by a generator. They sat together on log benches my trail crew built with chainsaws years ago; we notched the sills, rounded the edges, sanded the tops. Now the benches were gray and weathered; they looked way more historic than they really are. Which is the opposite of these Stehekin neighbors, a generation or two older than us, all of whom look and act younger than they really are. Laurie begged off to join them, her work-worn wrists too fragile for dancing, while I had no such excuse. A friend grabbed my hand, and I was off.

We squared up, took one hand, then another, calloused and soft, and moved at the loud caller's direction. *Swing your partner.* A soft-bearded man in his twenties wore a large cross on a leather cord. *Swing your corner.* A seasonal ranger in a summer dress—this, a rare excuse to wear one—laughed and twirled. *Promenade.* I danced three rounds then sneaked off. When I ducked behind a tree to pee, a rattlesnake gave a half-hearted warning and slunk back into the brush. I caught my breath and gazed up through the tangle of limbs at the omnipresent smoke, listened to laughter, the high strains of a fiddle, the bossy loud caller, the generator hum. I should get back, I knew. I stared up, instead, at ghostly unseen stars.

A few months earlier. The underground tour began in a room of mannequins at a faux saloon. They were white men, all of them, and they sat at round tables playing cards, whiskey bottles at their elbows, awkwardly positioned, the plastic legs not meant for sitting, elbows not meant to bend, like Barbie dolls. A couple of them looked eerily familiar: one smirked like John Wayne; another lifted his eyebrows like Vincent Price. All the mannequins wore cowboy hats except John Wayne, who wore a derby, and one—Daniel Boone?—who sported a coonskin cap. Most wore bandannas around their necks, a few wore vests. Were they repurposed? Shipped from a movie set or art installation? Wherever they came from, they landed in Pendleton, Oregon, fifty miles south of Walla Walla, to tell a campy tale: high jinks in the underground saloon!

Pendleton is best known for the annual Round-Up, a rodeo that attracts thousands of visitors each summer, and for the Pendleton Woolen Mill, whose famous plaid shirts and blankets fetch a dear price both new and used. For years, in my hometown in California, friends collected the shirts at garage sales and resold them at thrift shops for a pretty profit. There are more saddle shops in downtown Pendleton than you'll find in a three-state radius, and there are dozens of bars, some still called saloons, one Mexican restaurant, heavy on the cheese, and two Chinese places: Jade Garden and Golden Fountain. A railroad follows a river through town, and it's a very long way to the city. Two hundred miles to Portland or Boise. Two seventy-five to Seattle.

The Pendleton Underground was discovered in the late 1980s when locals began to see potholes crack open in downtown streets. Excavation uncovered a whole series of tunnels and rooms, which clever entrepreneurs filled with mannequins and artifacts. Now for fifteen bucks, you can take a two-hour tour, and on a Sunday in February, twenty-five or so tour takers took the bait, including my brother's family on vacation from New Jersey, Laurie, and me. We had planned to go cross-country skiing. We drove through undulating hills of winter wheat, brilliant new green against the white sky, and into the snowy Blue Mountains, past an oven, an actual oven, left outside, its door wide open on the side of the road with a stolen road sign atop, Open Range—meant to be taken literally, apparently, but not seriously—until the unplowed snow on the road piled six inches deep. Then we turned around.

We landed underground, standing awkwardly, looking around at our fellow tour takers, every one of whom wore the same expression in the faux saloon: for this we paid fifteen bucks? But things soon got more interesting, and this, to be honest, is why I had wanted to take the tour. From the saloon, the guide took us through dank hallways, under low ceiling beams—beefy, exposed, and shored up—and past an array of faux businesses: a laundry, butcher, an apothecary, and an ice-cream shop, all of them run in the old days, according to lore, by Chinese immigrants.

Check out Yelp in advance of your trip to the Pendleton Round-Up or stumble upon a column in the regional airline magazine, and here's what you'll learn: the Pendleton Underground was constructed because in the late 1880s and 1890s Chinese residents had a curfew that required them to be indoors after six. They'd been laborers on the railroad, but the railroad had been completed. They'd been gold miners, but the gold was played out. They'd moved into this small town and others around the West, and they weren't exactly welcome. The curfew was one of countless efforts to make life miserable enough for them to leave: taxes, restrictions on movement and marriage. Life wasn't easy for the Chinese residents of Pendleton, our tour guide lamented, but underground, at least, they could move freely.

Or just sleep. We soon entered a bunkhouse with tiny cots in a row. Off to the side sat a dark closet-like space that may have been an opium den, but even the opium intrigue couldn't distract us from the cots, cramped and close. The tour guide explained that Chinese workers averaged between four foot eight and five foot two and weighed an average of one hundred pounds.

I fidgeted with annoyance, trying to maintain touristy detachment. But, really. How can you offer this tour and barely explain why the Chinese community needed to build tunnels underground, much less condemn it? Noodle around in history, a half step past Yelp reviews, and you discover pretty quickly there was no Chinese curfew, not officially, not legally. The 1870 census shows Chinese people living above ground in Pendleton operating businesses like anyone else. But God knows there was violence, always violence, and the violence got worse when cowboys got drunk after dark. The point of this tour, though, was not to make a big deal about persecution. The tour was entertainment, plain and simple. Or mostly. In the room just past the bunkhouse, a map on the wall showed Japanese Fu-Go balloons launched during WWII intending to set fire to Northwest forests. Kept secret by the US government for years, the locations of remains of the balloons, which landed all around the Pacific Northwest, are mapped on the wall.

After an hour or so, we followed a narrow staircase to a faux brothel. This, and not the oppressed men, was the main draw in the tour. Chinese people weren't the only ones moving freely underground. The tunnels had secret entrances. A man in the John Wayne era could step out for a smoke and end up playing cards in a saloon with a Daniel Boone look-alike or sneak upstairs to the brothel, or for that matter, chill in the opium den, and no one would be the wiser. We toured the brothel, drank a paper cup of high-end hot chocolate, and wound through a small room with some miscellaneous relics: coins, pipes, a handful of opium pillows.

Only the gift shop remained, crowded enough to draw the attention of a fire marshal. You could buy yo-yos, playing cards, plastic dinosaurs, a shot glass with a picture of a bull rider, hat in hand, bucking away. You could also take photos, as we all did, putting your faces in cutout faces of bare-legged whores beside a very short man with a very tall cowboy hat, the oversized barrel of his pistol aimed at the camera. The Old West, the Wild West, the goofy goofy West! But even if you were to purchase one of a half dozen books for sale on local history and lore, you wouldn't find a single sentence about Chinese people.

The wooden plank floors creaked as tour takers elbowed toward the cash register. I was busy trying to stay out of the fray, so it took a while before I noticed animals all around me. Deer and elk, yes, yes, sure, but also foxes, eagles, bobcat, a cougar, a grizzly bear, a mountain goat. They were, frankly, awesome. To see their actual size, their actual fur, their eyes, making contact. I am never sure when I encounter taxidermy creatures how to react. To be so close spurs wonder, and underneath it, grudgingly, admiration for the artistry. How did they get the details just right? At some point, though, admiration turns to outrage: Who the hell killed these beautiful animals?

At the square dance, I found a group of friends leaning against a battered pickup in the dark and joined them sipping whiskey from a small flask. One dance ended and another began. Eventually I was pulled back in. This dance was more complicated than earlier ones. Take your left hand over his left shoulder—and who is "he" again?—and duck underneath, but don't let go. Together you turn your square inside out, and then right yourselves again.

We tried and got it wrong. We laughed and tried again.

Sometimes smoke settles so thick and omnipresent you forget it's there. In 1889, Alfred Downing, an explorer and illustrator who'd served on an early expedition through these mountains, returned to find the valley ablaze. He described how the fires raged: "Fanned by a northwest wind, the fire ran up both sides of the canyon to the very summits with the speed of a hurricane, accompanied by terrific crackling and roaring." As I danced my mind wandered. Chee Saw would have seen fire dribble down a mountainside, torch a creekside fir, then race upward through dry crowns to the ridge top. He would've breathed dense smoke. I imagined him on a night like this: a spatter of raindrops, the stars obscured, river water lapping, and laughter, too, and music. I felt a warm rush of kinship.

Another small town, another mannequin. The museum, in Pateros, fifteen miles upstream from Chelan Falls, is very small, housed in a side room in a small building that also houses city hall on Main Street, set back from the Columbia by a couple hundred feet. Two years earlier, Pateros almost burned to the ground in the massive Carlton Complex fire. Many houses were lost. Residents were displaced. As a result, when I visited, the museum was a bit disordered. Displays had been packed up for evacuation, then partially re-presented. Black-and-white photos on the wall showed Fourth of July parades and jet boat races, pioneers in top hats and corseted dresses, framed apple box labels.

But at the center of the room? Standing before a painted mural backdrop in a baggy white shirt and a wide-brimmed hat, with a thin moustache and a long queue: a Chinese miner. In front of him sat a rocker, a near-perfect replica from what I could tell, the first I'd seen in real life. The Chinese miner looked like he stayed in place during the evacuation. His plastic limbs hadn't been manipulated like the saloon-sitters in Pendleton. He was a survivor, this miner.

Mannequins are low budget, yes, and out of date, from another era. They're campy and creepy, the stuff of *Twilight Zone* episodes. In another, more academic setting you could name the effect as "othering." But here, even more than in Pendleton, the intention felt deadly earnest. He wasn't a repurposed Disney figure playing a game of poker. He was working. He seemed, dare I say, real. He wasn't a likeness of Chee Saw, since Chee Saw was a merchant not a miner, but he could have been one of the Chinese miners whose names survived the sieve of history.

He may have represented Tue Yu, among the earliest settlers in the Pateros area, who stayed after the Chinese miners exited and according to one newspaper account established "many lifelong friendships." Or maybe Chin Lee, who held claims near Rock Island. Or perhaps Ah Tai (Wong Fook Tai) who emigrated from China in 1877 at age seventeen, and lived in a "primitive, earth-covered dugout shelter on a barren gravelly river flat above the banks of the Columbia River." He'd come from Southern China to Portland, on a ship at the cost of twenty-five dollars, and headed upriver then overland to Wallace, Idaho, where he met up with his brother, Ah Nem, and their uncle, Chin Jim. In the early 1900s, according to Esvelt, the amateur historian, they ran a little store from a log cabin that sold "dry goods, dishes, medicines, fruits, firecrackers, and Chinese novelties" to white settlers who considered the place a "curiosity shop." Whoever the mannequin was supposed to be, he stood tall—way taller than five foot two—and his position of prominence delighted me.

A few feet from the display, a door ajar led me down a hall-way, which was once the town jail, where I could see through a door of metal bars into four small cells, each smaller than a dressing room stall at JCPenney, one of which was filled with taxidermy animals stacked willy-nilly, one upon the next. When the fire came close, the animals ended up in the jail cells. Who-ever put them there had a sense of humor: some faced forward, one had a paw raised, claws forward, as though a wild animal party got out of hand, and the cougars and bear cubs ended up in the drunk tank, still half-sloshed, to dry out for the night.

The ways white people characterize ourselves in the West are complicated: prideful, joyous, perplexing, infuriating. We want to honor our heritage, but can't seem to define it coherently or cohesively. We haven't been here long enough, apparently, to be sure. When I turn to the dictionary for help, I'm taken aback. The original definition of "heritage" from the Old French *her-itor*, is all about property being kept in the family, inherited, a notion that feels exclusive at best and greedy at worst, but can't be ignored.

So, at last, I looked up my own. It was surprisingly easy. My people come from County Galway, Ireland, and from Hanover, Germany, and from Salerno, Italy, and if my last name, Spagna, is any indication, from Spain before that. (My mother harbors a theory that this could mean they were displaced Jews, but they've long since identified as Catholic.) They arrived in the United States between the years 1875 and 1900, and they farmed and worked in steel mills and started businesses. Like most immigrants, they were probably persecuted, and as white people in America, they probably did some persecuting. Though if they did, like most people with an ounce of shame or self-preservation, they left no written record of it. Which isn't to say no record exists. My grandfather, according to articles saved in a scrapbook, pretended to be "Joby Riba, Heap Big Indian" who could not speak English, in order to play professional football while simultaneously playing as an amateur at Lehigh. Sixty years later, I inherited money from his widow, a second wife, a woman I never met. That inheritance enabled Laurie and me, as part-time seasonal laborers, to buy land.

On Sundays, across the river from our house in Stehekin, some locals shoot guns. Religion dictates a day of rest. You're not supposed to work, but it's okay to shoot. That's leisure. We'd hear it all afternoon, all over the valley: bang bang bang bang bang. A friend who's a Vietnam vet once asked them to ease up, told them the shooting brings back bad memories. They didn't stop. It's their constitutional right, and you get used to it after a while. Bang bang bang bang bang bang.

Close the windows. Get back to work.

Hard as we work, everyone agrees, the old-timers worked harder. They were hardy, super hardy. In Stehekin, people have clung to some of that hardiness, though with each generation some is slipping away. First came cars, then chainsaws, electricity, now the internet, every bit of it making life too easy, and over time, during the months I was busy thinking about Chee Saw, a kind of panic began to emerge, a sense of impending siege. Not that we'd fall to annihilation by climate change, which seemed very likely to me. Nor that we'd see the second coming of Christ, which seemed more likely to some. But the vague sense that someone from somewhere else was going to take over. In 2016, at the Malheur National Wildlife Refuge in Oregon—450 miles south of us, a long way away, but not long enough—gun-toting white men took over government offices because, they said, the government had taken over their land. Many in the West cheered their actions as heroism.

The most famous Chinese massacre in the American West occurred in Rock Springs, Wyoming, in 1885. Twenty-eight Chinese people were murdered and many more injured. Their houses were burned to the ground. In the aftermath, survivors realized with horror that the perpetrators had been people they knew well, including a white woman who had been their English teacher.

Poet Teow Lim Goh has written movingly about the event. In "Chinatown Burning," she imagines the night from various perspectives, including a schoolteacher sifting through loot in the aftermath and testifying to a jury that the Chinese burned their own houses down because "They were afraid white men would find their money." Hers was hardly the only chilling betrayal. In *The Chinese Must Go: Violence, Exclusion, and the Making of the Alien in America*, Beth Lew-Williams explains that workingmen's newspapers around the West "cast the incident as a justifiable reaction against the urgent threat of Chinese migration."

I was not histrionic enough to think gun-rights proponents would go so far as to murder someone like me for being a woman or queer or an environmentalist. I was not even ready to believe—or I remained too naïve to believe—they would kill immigrants or Black people, but they were undeniably ready for any threat to their property or identity, and their readiness, frankly, scared me.

The music was still playing—an agile fiddle, a steady guitar—and the caller was still calling, but I'd had enough. I searched around in the smoky dark to find Laurie, to find our car. The fire was burning ten miles away. It would burn until snowfall, likely as not. On the horizon, over the dark fringe of treetops, you could see a halo of orange. The flames remained out of view. When Alfred Downing left the valley in 1889 on the ferry, he missed the scenery, he said, "on account of the density of the smoke, which appeared to cover the face of the whole country." Now history was repeating itself. Fire managers assured us, over and over: the mountain burned so recently and so hot we ought to be safe this time. Still, it was hard to take a deep breath.

Chapter Thirteen
BACK TO THE STORE

I turned down the winding entry drive to find Beebe Bridge Park awash in color: grass irrigated green, hillsides brushed dull yellow, maples orange, and then there's the sky, a deep autumn hue, cornflower or dusty sapphire. The morning was cold, the upper twenties, colder than expected at the tail end of October, so I stopped at Kelly's Ace Hardware to buy a warm hat since I'd left mine at home. Now I sat in my Honda waiting with the heater running as a utilities crew passed by hauling pipes and hand tools, working to close things down on this, the last day of the season. A bitter wind blew, and in the empty campground it wasn't hard to picture Chee Saw buttoning up, preparing for winter. Wood to stack, root crops to store, boats to haul ashore. The river eased past the confluence with the Chelan River, swollen but benign, swirled on the surface. I could see across the wide expanse to the cantilevered rock where Dave Clouse's friend died, the place where I first imagined the massacre occurred, back when I thought pinpointing the massacre site and determining the details would be easy. Or at least not impossible.

A small sedan pulled into the empty spot next to mine. Since the last time I saw Dorothy Petry, in Chesaw, we'd stayed in touch, but I'd had little to report. I'd talked to scholars writing about the Chinese elsewhere in the West who'd never heard of

Chelan Falls. I'd hired a student to pore through the journals Dorothy lent me of an early county commissioner: nothing. Now here she was, waving exuberantly from the passenger seat, accompanied by her daughter, Ellen, and Kay and Mike Sibley, all veterans of the grave-dowsing day. They'd driven four hours straight from Oroville, stopping only for donuts and restrooms. They'd brought maps and documents, a new walker for Dorothy.

Dorothy stepped out of the car wearing layers, a sweater, a heavy vest, and a purple down coat with a hood she'd rarely pull up, despite the cold. The first order of business, from Dorothy's perspective, was to fix the exact location of Chee Saw's store. She had two survey maps in the basket on her walker, one from 1880, the other from the archaeological dig on which the archaeologist, Vicki, encountered the ghost children.

"We'll start near the bathrooms," she said.

She set off, pushing the wheeled walker fast across the asphalt, and Ellen ran after her. If she hit a crack or a stretch of downhill, there could be trouble.

Dorothy moved steadily and reached into her pocket for the crystal.

The bathrooms occupy a bland cinder block building in the center of the campground halfway between the river and the highway. I'd showered there more times than I cared to remember, paying with a stack of quarters inserted one at a time. When the hot water stops, you have to pay again, shivering naked, shampoo in your eyes, a makeshift process requiring stubborn agility, not unlike the kind Dorothy exhibited as she gazed around at the river, the lawns, the trees, getting her bearings, then stilled herself. Her small hand, thin-fingered, tremored slightly. She draped the gold chain lightly over her right forefinger and gripped the slack against her palm. I jammed my hands in the pockets of my coat, gazed up at the yellow bluffs, watched white clouds scooting slow. A chain-link fence was the only boundary between the park and semitrucks roaring past at breakneck speed, empty trailers swaying dangerously in the wind. Dorothy asked a series of questions about the store's location, whether it moved because of the earthquake (YES) then homed in on the timeline. What year did Chee Saw arrive at this place? This one required a series of follow-up questions. Was it before 1850 or after? Before 1860 or after? And so on until she landed on a firm date. Same process for when he left. He arrived, she determined, definitively, in 1857. He left in 1878.

The answers again gelled precisely with what I'd so far deduced. If Chee Saw is Ah Chee on the 1878 census at thirty-eight, and he arrived in 1857, he arrived at age seventeen. Possible. If he stayed after the massacre, but left in 1878, that matches the timeline for Chee Saw's arrival up north exactly. The earthquake played a role? Check.

I fought a growing sense of unease in facing the truth: storytelling casts a spell. Our public mythologies like our personal mythologies have roots in reality, but they're fertilized by faith. If I let myself think too much about the irony—how closely the work I do at the keyboard mirrors Dorothy with her crystal—I might've felt depressed or defeated, but we had no time for reflection.

Dorothy kept trying to pin down the location of the other structures in the Chinese village. Were there others? YES, across the highway, especially. This made sense because the grade starts to slope upward toward the cliffs, and the stables, according to the 1892 *Spokesman* article, were dug into the ground with the roof at ground level. Dorothy reveled in this kind of on-the-ground speculation, and she was nothing if not detail-oriented. She asked questions rapid-fire, but none addressed what I really wanted to know.

I finally interrupted to point out the cantilevered rock.

"I've been wondering," I said. "Maybe that's where the massacre took place? Can you ask?"

She pursed her lips, deciding how to phrase the question.

Can we see a massacre site from here? (NO) She was frustrated but undeterred. The answer, obviously, would be to move to a different sightline, so Dorothy took a beeline down a paved path heading straight to the river, before Ellen raced ahead, put her body in front of the walker to stop momentum, and reminded Dorothy to be more careful. Dorothy laughed and asked the crystal a couple more times if we could see the massacre site from here. (NO) She moved. From here? (NO) From here? (NO) Ellen worried about her mother standing so long and urged her to sit on the walker's fold-down seat. Dorothy sat and tried the question with verbal geographic cues, and the answers began to shift toward the affirmative. Is the massacre upriver? (YES) Is it downriver? (YES) Is it across the river? (YES)

These sounded, at best, like false positives. Unless…

Was there more than one massacre? YES

We returned to the cars in silence; all giddiness had seeped away. Still, I persuaded them to check out a few other sites before lunch downtown and their four-hour drive home. I drove alone in one car, ten minutes from Beebe Bridge to Chelan while the radio reported news of an impeachment trial impending, a World Series heading to a seventh game, and 475,000 migrant families arrested, nearly four times as many as the year before. I listened with dismay as I looked for the Beebe Springs trailhead, so unobtrusive as to be nearly hidden, at the end of the last switchback before reaching Chelan.

The small parking lot was empty, but Mike and Kay were jazzed by the discovery of this new hiking spot. They stepped away to read the interpretive signs: descriptions of the earthquake, the spring that spewed out of the ground, the restoration of the river below for salmon. The hike to the bluff would be short on a narrow rocky trail, but could not, in any way, accommodate a walker, so Ellen and Dorothy and I stood in the gravel lot, chins to our chests to avoid gusts of dust swirling in the wind. Was there a massacre here? (YES) How many were killed? More than twenty? (YES) More than thirty? (YES) All Chinese? (YES)

Kay and Mike returned from taking photos and admiring the views—the vast expanse of sky, the astonishing red locust crawling up the sides of narrow draws—and stood with us a few feet from the car where Dorothy had pulled her down coat tight around her with her left hand. We talked about how the water sprayed skyward right here in the wake of the earthquake and how the water itself could be a motivation. Of course, it could; water wars are more norm than exception in the West.

Dorothy's eyebrows remained scrunched in consternation. She was troubled, her ever-steady demeanor nearly shaken.

"There's something we aren't asking," she said.

So far I had avoided sharing the rest of the version of the story that unfolded at the Wanapum Heritage Center, but I could no longer see the point in holding back.

"Can you ask if any children were killed?"

Kay Sibley turned sharply. We'd never discussed the possibility, and it appeared in none of the written accounts. Dorothy pulled her lips tight as if in concentration.

Were any children killed? YES

Imagination crept in again, unbidden. The women tending crops in the wide flat expanse upriver of the Chinese store— corn, squash, potatoes, greens, herbs—stooped with seeds, tools in hand, brimmed hats on their heads, babies on their backs, and the older children helping plant or harvest, hauling water from the river, running, laughing, chasing geese or game, their skin sunbaked, their feet calloused. There's no high bluff close to the river, the killers would have to haul the bodies—so very light, hardly a burden—to the water's edge and toss them into the churn, the cruelty more than imagination wants to hold.

Deep sorrow seeped into the silent space between us.

"Should we take a drive?" I asked.

Dorothy did not miss a beat. "Yes, and this time I'll ride with you."

We followed Woodin Avenue past the Midtowner Motel, an osprey nest, a thrift store, and after the stoplight, the firehouse. The smooth lake stretched out toward the horizon where mountains knuckled in toward the lake, and the blue blue sky reached farther yet to Oroville, to Chesaw, to Canada. Dorothy's sadness was palpable. I pointed out the sights with strained enthusiasm, a new paved walking trail by the river lined by yellow-leaved cottonwoods, the Lake Chelan hydroelectric plant.

We left the pavement and rumbled onto the old stagecoach road I first drove with Dave and Sue Clouse more than two years earlier.

"It gets rough in spots," I said, and Dorothy guffawed.

A rough road couldn't rattle her, she said. Her father had been a customs officer near Chesaw, she said, and liked to drive out on Forest Service roads with the family. Her mom would get out and walk where it got steep or exposed. Dorothy was bolder, unworried by the fishtail of back tires on washboard or blind corners or the lack of guardrails. As our pace slowed, we lost the other car, for a time, in the rooster tail of dust kicked up in our wake.

Dorothy eased back into storyteller mode.

Had she ever told me she had an uncle who lived in Chesaw who taught her "Charlie" meant "Chinaman"? He'd known Charlie Chesaw personally. She talked about an ad she saw once for Chee Saw's store in a newspaper, maybe the *Omak Chronicle*—she was certain I'd seen it, but I insisted I hadn't—and she told me somewhere she heard Chee Saw entered the US on a boat down Okanogan River. He arrived when he was twenty-five and worked pulling green chain at a mill in Osoyoos, and that's where the "Saw" in his name originated. I'd never heard these stories, and they didn't fit with the timeline we'd just established back at the park, his arrival in 1857 at age seventeen, but none of this, I knew, was set in stone, it was all still conjecture.

We drove on until we reached the cantilevered rock from the day with Dave and Sue. The wind blew fiercely, and the spot was very exposed. I tried to urge Dorothy once again to sit in the car with the crystal, but she'd have none of it. She saw Kay and Mike and Ellen walking toward the edge, wowed by the view, and she headed straight toward them, without a walker, until Ellen caught her. She continued, then, holding onto Ellen's arm, but evidently without fear. The wind had picked up, so she held the white metal post of the danger sign and prepared to ask her crystal more questions.

Was there a massacre here? YES
Were they pushed? YES

So much wind. I'd left my new hat in the car, and even in the bright midday sun, I shivered. There were more questions to ask, more than 150 years' worth. But to what end? Dorothy's hands tremored wildly. Ellen suggested we stop, just stop. Dorothy met my gaze. I nodded once, and she pocketed the crystal resignedly, turned in place, a shuffled rotation, a slow three-sixty, as though she'd never see this place again, which she probably wouldn't, and began to walk slowly without a walker or an arm to hold to my car. She made it to the passenger seat and fumbled with the seat belt. I reached across to fasten it, and resisted the urge to pat her knee or shoulder with reassurance. I didn't want to risk being condescending. Instead, I started the engine, turned up the heater full blast, and idled to let the other car, this time, take the lead. I wanted to let the dust settle before we moved.

Dorothy fidgeted in her seat, rubbed one hand within the other, worked her jaw wordlessly. Not until she tried to speak did I realize she was crying.

Tragedy hung heavy between us. The children. The children. Kids who sneaked underfoot at the store, stole candies, or chewed ginger, rode horses or steered boats across the rapids, kids who should've watched the first steamboats arrive, the first bridge, the first World War, the Spanish flu. If they lived, they'd have been the age of my great-grandfather, not much older than Dorothy herself. We held their tissue-thin legacy in our hearts like dead weight. The road switchbacked steeply back toward the Columbia, then turned to pavement to take us through Chelan Falls, past the picker cabins, past abandoned fruit warehouses, across the Chelan River again, then upwards once more past Beebe Springs. We remained silent.

The Apple Cup Café was overcrowded for the lunchtime rush, so we settled with menus, seated in the empty cocktail lounge with Halloween decorations. Kay dove in, as she had in Chesaw, talking about similarities between how the Chinese were treated in the late nineteenth century and how Muslims and Mexicans are treated now. Yes, I said, yes, this kind of violent racism requires a group sensibility, but people can stand up against it.

"It takes courage," I said, and everyone nodded.

We chewed our sandwiches and returned to reminiscences of the area, better times, better memories, a lightening of the mood, like a boat coming into dock, slowing, steady, avoiding drift. Dorothy had come to Stehekin for her honeymoon. Kay once came on a high school trip. This place was theirs, too, and I reveled, for now, in the bond. When the time came for them to leave, I grabbed two boxes of organic apples from the orchard back home that I'd brought as gifts—meager since they have plenty of orchards where they live—and wedged them around the new walker in their trunk, and I handed Ellen a pie from the bakery in Stehekin, and gave hugs all around. They hit the road by 12:30, and I was alone again in town with streets named for the maybe murderers.

I took a long run along a trail on a high bluff in a cold wind nearly strong enough to knock me sideways as I watched the river unspool below me. I usually run with earbuds but not this time. No music, no NPR, no errands to run, no more returning to Walla Walla.

What filters through memory is the sound of Dorothy's voice dropping, worn away, sadly affected, and the long silence in the car when we turned into the draws in the hillside and back out, the sky broad and blue, not unlike the places she visited as a child, not unlike where Chee Saw roamed with winter approaching. Later, I'd think of our shared purpose as not unlike gold mining. We started with wild hope for a shiny nugget, a single answer. Instead we sluiced for dust, adding heavy shovelfuls of dirt, rocking it back and forth—not the kind of work you do alone—and collected some dust, barely enough to hold on the tip of a steak knife. And if we set everything we learned on a scale would it be worth anything?

I didn't know. I don't know.

Still, I hold the stories close as a whisper. I can't even hear the language they speak, not Syilx, not Cantonese, can't smell sweet opium or the sweat-soaked horses after a long ride through the coulees. I only have this: one last cold clear October day by the river. Quail coo and scatter. A kettle of vultures circles over the draws, too steep to see into. Once they find a carcass and descend, they will be called a wake.

PART III:
WHAT IF?

Chapter Fourteen
MASSACRE: VERSION III

A newspaper reporter stands alone in the ruins of the Chinese store. His head pounds steady as the wind-driven waves chopping at the shore, small price to pay for a night at the corner tavern and the tip that brought him here to the river's edge and this treasure trove of nostalgia. He's traveled to Chelan from Spokane, a thriving city of nearly twenty thousand souls 150 miles east, tasked with finding a new angle, something to stir interest in the region, draw more investors, settler-types, families. These ruins might fit the bill. He sits on a bedrock outcropping in shirt-sleeves soaking in spring sun, warmer than he'd expected, and he has to admit the ads he'd seen in the *Chelan Falls Leader* weren't as hyperbolic as he'd presumed. This is, indeed, fine country, ripe for cultivation. He taps his fountain pen on the warm rock to let flow the ink and dives in: *There are many tales of the unwritten history connected with the history of the Columbia River country all within sound of the gurgling water.* He drifts long on a raft of purple prose as he describes the old Chinese merchant, the lovesick gardener. But something's missing. Something more dramatic. He considers the recent unrest with the Chelan villagers. Nothing romantic about that. Suddenly he's got it. He gazes at the green bluffs across the river and reimagines the drama as he watches balsamroot flowers wave in the sun, watered by an underground spring. *The savages advanced cautiously and surrounded the celestials. It was an awful fight that sent terror into the hearts of Chinamen up and down the river.* Once he's finished, he slips off his shoes and wades into the water. He knows he's nailed it. Once he returns to the office, before the piece goes to print, he'll add the icing. *Not one remained to tell the tale.*

If you drive to Chelan from Chelan Falls, past All Season's Rentals and the high school football field (Go Mountain Goats!) and the Midtowner Motel, you follow Woodin Avenue. Woodin runs a straight-shot down from the bluffs overlooking the Columbia to the shore of Lake Chelan. On the horizon, mountaintops shine porcelain with sun-glazed snow. Clouds hover in brushstroke tapestry. Flowerpots hang from light posts over benches by an espresso shop. All of it well-tended, tourist-focused. One more block and you reach the lakeshore, obscured now by Campbell's Resort, the oldest hotel and convention center in the state. Right here is where the Chelan villagers took their stand.

Seventeen years passed between 1875, the year of the Chelan Falls massacre, and 1892, the year the *Spokesman* article appeared—the *only* article to report the event, if report is even the right word. To call these years "eventful" in the West would be ridiculous understatement. They're years bookended by infamous conflicts. Little Bighorn in 1876, Wounded Knee in 1891. Native people defeated Custer at Little Bighorn. The US Army took revenge at Wounded Knee. The history is nowhere near that simple in the broad sense, nor does it unfold tidily on Lake Chelan.

In 1879, when President Rutherford B. Hayes created the so-called Moses Reservation, including nearly all of Chelan and Okanogan Counties, the US Army set up a post—Camp Chelan—in the fall and abandoned it within a year. In short order, the boundaries of the reservation shifted east, but the new legislation allowed local tribes to claim allotments along the north shore of Lake Chelan. Some Entiats, including Chee Saw's old friend Wapato John, claimed hundreds of acres. Most Chelans, however, refused to move off land they considered their own, land closer to the end of the lake. In 1886, the government opened up this former (short-lived) reservation land to white settlers. In 1888, Lewis H. Woodin started a lumber mill. Chelan men helped carry the gear including an eight-thousand-pound boiler up the steep stagecoach road.

Tensions grew taut. The town site was set to be platted right where members of the Chelan band held their ground—right where Woodin Avenue runs into Campbell's Resort today—on the shore of the clear blue lake, where Chief Innomoseecha Jim, often called "Long Jim" for his height, over six feet, and his straight-backed bearing, lived in what Steele's 1906 *History of North Central Washington* calls a "beautiful home." By day, government officials pounded survey stakes. By night, Chelan people pulled them out. They weren't leaving. They weren't even followers of Chief Moses, who had negotiated supposedly on their behalf. They were separate people, sovereign, independent. Chief Long Jim insisted his father, Innomoseecha, hadn't signed any treaty. He filed a lawsuit along with Cultus Jim and Chelan Bob and testified in court, "Moses and I were not friends. Moses kept all the money for himself, which he got from the Government for the land."

Cultus Jim and Chelan Bob, for their part, lived at the mouth of the Chelan River directly across from the Chinese store. In court, they cited improvements they'd made to their respective properties in accordance with the Homestead Act. They'd built cabins, stables, fences. They'd planted trees. One county auditor asserted that together the two men cultivated over forty tons of hay. By any measure, they had "proved up." Nevertheless, a white man named A. W. LaChapelle put down stakes on their land drawn by the allure of Beebe Springs, still flowing, making this parcel far more valuable than some plats in town, still dry, near desert. It is hard to picture how, exactly, this went down.

Did LaChapelle move in while Cultus Jim and Chelan Bob were off hunting? Did he drive them off with weapons or threats and refuse to let them return? Whatever the case, LaChapelle called a local Indian agent and had Cultus Jim and Chelan Bob arrested for trespassing. They were, he said, "dangerous characters." The two men went to jail.

But the story doesn't end there. One high-ranking official, R. W. Starr, head of the land office in nearby Waterville, defended the Native people. He argued on their behalf in the *Big Bend Empire*: "They testified that their father's fathers had land there for generations. The whites only came in 1890. Prior to that time the rights of the Indians had been respected by whites for half a century, the Indians refusing tempting offers to buy them off." His defense predictably infuriated some white men in Chelan.

On January 8, 1891, seventeen "civic leaders" from Chelan signed a letter to the editor of the *Spokane Falls Review*, which had reprinted the *Empire* piece, a rebuttal full of simmering umbrage. The letter begins politely enough: "The settlers are conscientious. They feel that the Indians have forfeited all their rights, and that they belong on the reservation where they can take allotments if they so desire." But soon the writer cuts to the chase. "Would it not be more credible for the people to assist in ridding our community of shiftless savages who have never cultivated to exceed fifteen acres and that in the most disgraceful manner? With rich soil and water flowing at their command, they simply insulted nature." The names of several of the signatories, including Lewis Woodin and C. C. Campbell, grace prominent signs and businesses in Chelan today.

Still, the story did not end. In 1891, another white man, a US Indian inspector named Robert S. Gardner, stepped in. "I cannot conscientiously recommend their removal," he wrote, "but respectfully recommend that they be recognized and treated as non-reservation Indians, that they be allowed their lands." The standoff would simmer for several more years.

*

Whether the unnamed reporter knew all of this, we can't say, but he would know, for sure, which side of the dispute to land on. Casting Indigenous people as "savages" who'd massacred hapless Chinese could help justify stealing their land. The writer may not have made the calculation so baldly. When do we ever? We weigh costs and, more often than not, choose to swim in the current of the ideology we inhabit, even when—especially when—we don't even recognize we're inhabiting one. This writer may have been a young newcomer or a hardened Civil War veteran, a newly arrived immigrant or a son of privilege. Almost certainly, he hailed from the East. Few white men born on the frontier had yet grown to working age. His paper, the *Spokesman*, had just merged with the *Spokane Falls Review*, and the new owner, Frank Dallam, grew the thriving business enough to build a downtown tower so impressive eight thousand people showed up for a tour when it opened.

Maybe the writer never comes to Chelan at all. Say, he sits in an office in the tall new office building, dips his pen in ink. He's seen abandoned camps where Chinese placer miners once lived; they're all over the place in nearby Idaho. He's read about murders of Chinese people, and the details are easy enough to evoke. He never specifies the number of dead, never uses the word *massacre*. He conjures the gruesome story from thin air, and ends on hopeful note: *Now the placer fields of the past are owned by settlers and are fast becoming beautiful fruit orchards.*

Chapter Fifteen
NEARLY UNANIMOUS

On a summer afternoon, Keith Carpenter and I sat at a picnic table by the bakery, the only must-stop establishment in Stehekin. Above us, a steep tower of granite—Tupshin Peak—leaned its shadow across a forested slope. Beside us, sprinklers turned in a wide lazy arc over a pasture. Before us: hot coffee and cinnamon rolls. Keith's family once owned the orchard Laurie maintains, so we'd known each other in passing for a long time. Gray-bearded, broad-shouldered, and good-natured, he is the grandson of people who arrived in the Chelan area around the turn of the twentieth century. They bought land, grew apples, raised their children, just as Keith, too, stayed put, owned an orchard and the rental shop at a tiny single-lift ski area outside of town where he taught lessons to kids. When he was young, his family lived on a small drive-to island in the Columbia River, and they'd see depressions where the Chinese miners lived in half-buried dwellings to avoid the heat, and they'd see hollows in the riverbank where the miners dug out gravel to sluice. They'd find coins on occasion, buttons, baubles, evidence of Chinese people up and down that river stretch, yes, of course, and he's heard they were good at what they did, found gold where the whites found none. Keith's stories spooled out easy as late-day sun through the sprinkler haze, one leading to another to another.

Before we parted ways, I asked him one question: Did he

know any descendants of the Chinese? Any at all? He shook his head with regret.

"The massacre," he said.

"It happened for sure?" I asked.

"How else did they disappear?"

I didn't know. But I did know the story was messy.

One day back when I was scrolling through microfilm in the basement of the library at Whitman College, I discovered an editorial from the *Chelan Falls Leader* published on August 13, 1891, titled simply, "No Chinese." There will "never be any room in Okanogan County and especially in Chelan Falls for Chinese," it read. The racist sentiment seemed disgraceful, but common enough, and therefore unremarkable to me at the time. But after talking with enough people who ascribed their full-scale departure to the massacre, the date stood out. If the Chinese population left in the wake of an 1875 massacre, left so fast their homes rotted with possessions in place, why did the editors of the *Chelan Falls Leader* oppose them with such fervor some sixteen years *after* the event?

"While Uncle Sam's body politic has digested and assimilated some pretty tough morsels of foreign population," the editorial board wrote, "the heathen Chinese is altogether too much for him and dyspepsia has ensued."

Dyspepsia? They are physically sickened? This isn't language you use for people long since gone; it could not be farther from the language in the *Spokesman* article, which would appear less than a year later. In fact, the *Spokesman* article itself shows at least one timeline crack. The writer claims, "Here was also a store that five years ago carried a larger stock than any white man's enterprise in Okanogan, Lincoln, or Douglas Counties." Five years ago? From 1892? As in 1887? A dozen years after the massacre? The store not only existed, but was thriving?

This version of the story aligns with a few others. Marjorie Pattie McGrath's memoir, *Pioneer in Pigtails*, about growing up in the 1880s on the Waterville Plateau above the Chinese store, includes warm reminiscences of her father, James Pattie, who traveled down to the store regularly to buy a particular hat he liked, straw and wide-brimmed, from a Chinese merchant with whom he was friendly. (The merchant apparently stuck around long enough for Mr. Pattie to wear through a few hats.) The merchant was likely not Chee Saw, who had long since moved up the Okanogan, but may have been a man named Que Yu, who is the subject of an oft-repeated story of kindness. Arnie Marchand writes a version in *The Way I Heard It.*

After the massacre, Marchand writes, most Chinese people deserted the village but a small number stayed on, ferrying people across the river, until 1895 when only one remained, a man by the name of Que Yu who lived at the site of the former store. One day, a local miner named James Mather was passing by and saw no smoke coming from the stovepipe, so he stopped and found Que Yu very sick. He boiled water and wrapped the man in wool blankets soaked in hot water until the fever broke. In exchange, once he recovered, Que Yu fixed Mather's rocker to allow him to sluice more effectively. Mather had until then been making one dollar every sixty days; afterwards he made "a phenomenal amount."

One thing seems clear: the massacre—if it happened— chased off some Chinese miners, but not all of them.

In the early 1890s, the region teetered on the brink of boom. Steamboats chugged upriver. The first ones made it to Wenatchee—the larger town where Chee Saw used to visit Sam Miller's trading post—by anchoring to the shore and winching their way through rapids and shoals, and they intended to go further, but the rugged forty-mile stretch between Wenatchee and Chelan Falls did not look promising. Meanwhile, after a lull caused by economic recession, the Great Northern Railway surveyed a route from Spokane to Seattle that ran straight through Wenatchee. The town was quickly surveyed with substantial help from the railroad company, and within five days of completion on May 6, 1892, more than $100,000 worth of real estate sold.

Smack in the middle of this wild growth spurt, on March 8, 1892, a meeting was convened to consider the potential expulsion of Chinese people from the newly drawn town limits. "The attendance was large," according to the Steele history, "and personnel represented citizens both in and out of the city." While there was "no desire for mob violence," the crowd wanted to "deport the celestials." Not merely exclude them, but kick them out. Why bother if there were hardly any left?

Maybe they weren't so worried about the existing Chinese population as the potential for newcomers. The railroad—source of wealth and prosperity though it was—posed the problem. More than ten thousand Chinese laborers had famously worked on the Central Pacific Railroad out of Sacramento that connected with the Union Pacific when the golden spike was driven on May 10, 1869. Another two thousand worked on the Northern Pacific Line on the west side of the Cascades, from Kalama north to Tacoma, completed in 1873. The Chinese miners who'd settled along the Columbia in North Central Washington lived in small groups and worked independently. Perhaps, in the kind of calculation that so often accompanies xenophobia, the miners represented "good" Chinese, while the railroad workers on the horizon would be "bad."

The clamor for exclusion reflected the broader political climate. While anti-Chinese fever abated in San Francisco after Denis Kearney's demise and quieted in the wake of expulsive riots in Tacoma and Seattle, east of the Cascades incidents were still on the rise. In 1887, the Hells Canyon Massacre took place, and the same year, a fire ravaged all the Chinese businesses in Walla Walla. The violence inched closer, which both increased fear and gave broad license to the white citizens.

Whatever the reason, the meeting in Wenatchee was convened, and a committee of six was elected to make sure no

Chinese person would be allowed to locate within the town limits. In the midst of discussions, an obvious point arose: How? How would they get them out and/or keep them out? The attendees agreed, in principle, that they intended to use "legal, honorable, and lawful means" but if these didn't work, "another mass meeting could easily be assembled and the committee urged to adopt other methods."

At this point in the proceedings, a lone voice rose in opposition. A man named Noah N. Brown rose to speak at length against the wisdom of exclusion. His words do not remain, but his arguments can be gleaned from voices that defended Chinese communities all over the West. They worked hard! They did nothing wrong!

Would the writer of the *Spokesman* article have known about this meeting? Probably. It was widely reported. If he fabricated or exaggerated the massacre, why should we presume he did so in order to defame the Indigenous people, to cast or recast them as villains? Why presume he was on the side of the vested interests? Have writers never advocated for the underdog, the oppressed, the so-called voiceless? Maybe his focus was on the Chinese. Maybe by romanticizing the merchant and the miners and the lovesick gardener, he offered subversive support to the Chinese people who remained.

For that matter, why presume the writer was a man? The article was written in an era when new technology allowed newspapers to boom and, often enough, to hire women. The Pacific Coast Women's Press Association held its first conference in 1891. By 1900, there would be more women's bylines in American newspapers than men's, and while most were relegated to the popular "ladies" pages, writing recipes and gossip, often under pseudonyms, others were successful travel writers like Isabella Bird, whose 1879 *A Lady's Life in the Rocky Mountains* became an instant bestseller (and a timeless favorite, savored by many outdoorsy friends, both men and women, I worked with over the years) or Mary Roberts Rinehart, who traveled through Chelan and Stehekin to pen *A Chronicle of Sport and Adventure in Glacier Park and the Cascade Mountains* in 1917. Other daring investigators went undercover to expose corruption or injustice, like Nellie Bly who famously faked mental illness in 1887 to write *Ten Days in a Mad House* or Teresa Dean, a *Chicago Herald* reporter and a young divorcée, who showed up at Wounded Knee to bear witness to the atrocities. If the *Spokesman* reporter had a political bent, in addition to her obvious flair for the dramatic, she may have wanted to expose mistreatment of Chinese immigrants.

If she wanted to press the point, casting them as victims of horrific violence—*easy prey for their savage antagonists*—could drive the point home. But she wouldn't want to push too hard, wouldn't want to suggest they had been the victims of white people. No reader likes to be called racist. And hadn't the men in Wenatchee at least emphasized "legal means"? No, the hardworking beloved storekeeper and his lovesick gardener, these simple hardworking people, had been the victims of "savages." What civilized white man, what would-be city founder, would choose to be associated with that behavior? Who would want to repeat it? The unnamed reporter may have been putting her prose on the side of Noah N. Brown, whose own story is less elusive.

Like many men of the era, Brown lived a wide-ranging life. (Funny how men in nearly constant motion are so often called "settlers.") He bought a hotel in Wenatchee in 1891, sold it after sixteen months and went to the World's Fair in Chicago, then bought himself a sled dog team and headed north to mine gold on the Yukon River. He took forty-three days to get to Nome with his dog team and lasted only a couple of seasons before returning to Wenatchee. Why did he leave in the first place?

Wanderlust? Or was a hotel just not profitable in those early years? Is it possible he left because he was disgusted with the treatment of Chinese immigrants? Or because he was ostracized for taking a stand? Perhaps. But he returned in 1903 and by 1906 had taken his place, or retaken it, as a model citizen, described as "fully deserving of the prominent position which he holds and the esteem and confidence so generously bestowed by this host of friends." His name, at any rate, remains in the history books, in a full-page biography in *History of North Central Washington* where his dissent at the anti-Chinese meeting is noted, as is the fact that after voicing his opposition, he did not vote no. A separate newspaper account affirms his retreat: "A rising vote on the question of whether to exclude the Mongolians from town exhibited marked unanimity with only one man declining to come to his feet and even he refused to vote in the negative."

In a similar way, if the writer who memorialized the massacre story had hoped to make a difference on behalf of the Chinese community, she did not. Chinese people largely disappeared from the region as a result of political pressure or economic pressure or the insinuation of violence or, most likely, all of the above. They moved to the city or back to China or to Canada, or they married and assimilated into Native culture. In the end, the story—whether true or untrue or exaggerated—has done more harm than good.

The Chinese population can be written off with a fixed date attached, even though evidence for the massacre is scant. No legal records exist. No families came looking for bodies. There's no mention of the event in the colorful reveries of white cattlemen like Dan Drumheller or A. J. Splawn. Save Randy Lewis's corner tavern whispers, there are few rumors of perpetrators bragging as there were in Hells Canyon. There's no Native memory except that Cultus Jim and Chelan Bob were arrested, which is true, but not until fifteen years later and for defending their own land, not for killing Chinese miners. The Native people, in fact, hardly even bother to acknowledge the presence of Chinese people. In the ongoing legal battles to keep their land near Beebe Springs, Cultus Jim and Chelan Bob testified the whites had gotten along fine with them for "half a century." No mention of the Chinese miners. No mention of the store. Certainly no mention of a massacre. People only started talking about the massacre after the *Spokesman* hit the newsstand.

Writers have imaginations. Writers face deadlines. Writers can weave rumors into fact. Especially when there's no call to sign a byline. And in the process, an easy explanation is born.

Where did all the Chinese people go? They were massacred.

Chapter Sixteen
THE PROBLEM WITH
MAKE-BELIEVE

I was racing along the curvy road on the south shore of Lake Chelan trying to make the once-a-day ferry to Stehekin, when NPR hosts started discussing a massacre. In March 2019, a man armed to the teeth had entered two separate mosques in Christchurch, New Zealand, during Friday prayer and killed fifty-one people and injured forty-nine more. Months after the event, the motivation remained as clear as it was on Day One. The killer, a white supremacist, had posted hate-speech against Muslims on the internet and live-streamed the killings on Facebook. If you look up the event on Wikipedia, you'll find the heading "Christchurch mosque shootings," but that morning on NPR, the hosts were unequivocal, even casual, with use of the word *massacre*. And it made me wonder, as I had many times before, what qualifies as a massacre? What heinous detail spurs the upgrade?

On December 14, 2012, at Sandy Hook Elementary School in Newtown, Connecticut, twenty children and six adults were mowed down by a lone gunman. Something about the familiar moniker—"lone gunman"—feels off. The euphemism rightly obscures the identity of a murderer, but it also conjures the hero in a western, a victim outnumbered defending his honor or property. What on earth could a murderer at a grade school have been defending? You'll also find the event referred to, universally, as a "shooting." Why not "massacre"? Does there need to be more than one perpetrator? There wasn't in New Zealand.

Maybe a massacre requires a minority group of victims, some version of racism or xenophobia as motivation? The children in Newtown were mostly white, as was the killer. The young man apparently had all-purpose scorn for humanity. According to a 2014 *New Yorker* profile, he kept a spreadsheet with the specifics of four hundred incidents of mass violence dating back to 1786. Only in the final section of the profile does the word finally appear. "On the anniversary of the massacre..." it reads. Maybe it's all about distance. Maybe a killing only becomes a massacre in past tense, when the passage of time creates a glaze of unreality.

In the town of Almo, Idaho, some six hundred miles southeast of Chelan, a monument to a massacre sits on a street corner in a small patch of mown grass. The town sits equal distance, more or less, from Boise or Salt Lake City. Drive there from anywhere and you'll cross miles of mountains, farmland, deserts, exactly the kind of country hordes of wagon train emigrants crossed in the second half of the nineteenth century. As in so much of the West, this is the era to which most local history harkens. The words carved into a thin slab of polished granite read:

Almo, Idaho
Dedicated to the memory of those who lost their lives in a most horrible Indian massacre 1861
Three hundred immigrants west bound.
Only five escaped.
Erected by S&D [Sons & Daughters] of Idaho Pioneers 1938

Only problem is, it never happened.

Brigham D. Madsen debunked the story once and for all in a 1993 article titled "The 'Almo Massacre' Revisited" in the newsletter of the Idaho State Historical Society. The perpetrators were supposedly Shoshone men led by Chief Pocatello, and Madsen, a former University of Utah professor specializing in Indigenous history, would have none of it. The incident didn't show up in writing anywhere until Charles Walgamott's 1927 book *Reminiscences of Early Days: A Series of Historical Sketches and Happenings in the Early Days of Snake River Valley.* Any massacre that large, Madsen argues, would have been reported in the California newspapers since that's where the travelers were headed. His dismissal is full-throated. "When even the slightest Native American disturbance along the road received immediate notice from these various western newspapers, the lack of any reference to an affair at Almo Creek can only mean that there was no 'Almo Massacre,'" he writes.

Madsen suspects a local newspaperman hyped the story in the 1930s as a way to bring attention to nearby City of Rocks, known for its high desert nature and tall granite spires, and maybe get it designated a national monument. Locals coveted the tourist dollars national parks attracted, and the campaign worked. Today City of Rocks is a national preserve, a popular destination for rock climbers and road trippers, and the massacre monument in Almo remains in place, despite the debunking, for all to see.

After Madsen's article appeared, the Idaho State Historical Society asked for the stone to be removed. Madsen lobbied for it to be replaced by a statue of Pocatello himself, though a representative of the Sons and Daughters of Idaho Pioneers admitted that replacement would be "hard to swallow." Meanwhile, members of the Shoshone-Bannock Tribes at nearby Fort Hall Indian Reservation called for a public apology. (There's been none.) All of this is reported online as fascinating trivia or click bait, and while some writers are indignant, the indignation itself can become an attraction. "Almo, Idaho boasts the most deceitful historical marker in the United States," writes historian James Loewen in his book *Lies Across America.* Business owners in Almo, for their part, don't seem to mind. They happily engage reporters and urge visitors to come see for themselves.

Not far from Almo sits Massacre Rocks State Park, which boasts disc golf and fifty RV sites and a narrow gap in the red rocks called "Gate of Death" or "Devil's Gate" where Native people might've ambushed a wagon train. But they didn't. Though this time, there's a grain of truth. Some ten miles east of the park, Shoshones did kill nineteen white travelers. "People love their massacres," my historian friend, Larry Cebula, had told me early in my research, and at some point I finally began to understand what he meant. For some tourist-seeking towns, any attention is good attention, yes, but more insidious reasons lurk just beneath the surface. In Southern Idaho, where the 2010 census found 95 percent of the population to be white, it matters that the victims of these made-up massacres were white. Those killed can either be held high as martyrs for the cause of Manifest Destiny or pitied as earnest bumblers who got what they deserved, a convenient sacrifice to a collective colonizers' guilt set safely in the long-ago.

And that's just the tip of the make-believe iceberg. But here's the problem: any analysis of fake massacres gets murky when you turn the phenomenon upside down to examine the *actual* massacres that have been buried or ignored. In most unreported or underreported massacres, Indigenous people are victims, not perpetrators. Historians have labored diligently to bring these stories to light. Consider the Bear Creek Massacre, also in Southern Idaho, thought to be the largest massacre of Native Americans in the West. On the morning of January 29, 1863, US Army Colonel Patrick O'Connor led his troops to annihilate between 244 and 493 men, women, and children, but it was more than one hundred years before Darren Parry, chairman of the Northwestern Band of the Shoshone Nation, a descendant of Chief Sagwitch who survived the massacre and lived to tell the tale, managed to bring the story to the attention of the National Park Service. The site was designated a National Historic Monument in 1990 and purchased outright by the Northwestern Band of the Shoshone Nation in 2018. Or consider the Sand Creek Massacre. On November 29, 1864, in Eastern Colorado, Colonel John M. Chivington and his troops killed 230 Cheyenne and Arapaho people, nearly all women and children. Alexa Roberts, the first superintendent of Sand Creek Massacre National Historic Site, which didn't open until 2014, boasted in *Smithsonian* magazine that it's the only NPS unit with *massacre* in its name. Then there's the Baker or Marias Massacre in Montana. In 1870, Colonel Eugene Baker led his troops along the Marias River upon a peaceful band of Blackfeet and murdered 37 men, 90 women, 50 children. By accident. They were the wrong band, but Baker reportedly said, "That makes no difference. One band or another of them…we will attack them." He also took 140 prisoners, but abandoned them when he realized many were sick with smallpox.

The numbers are all out of proportion: ten or twenty white people in the maybe massacres, a few hundred Indigenous people in the for-sure ones. And yet. To quantify them like this, to count bodies, risks allowing for perverse pleasure or even pride. All articles name the officials who committed the crimes, for example, but few if any of the victims. Even though these events took place in an entirely different historical context than contemporary mass shootings in which we refuse to name the "lone gunmen," naming the army guys, complete with rank, has a troubling whiff of glamorization. More dangerously, the sheer number of them, listed one after another after another, risks a shrug of dismissal or cowardly surrender as though horrific violence is simply human nature, the way of the world, inevitable.

Perhaps most crucially, as David Treuer argues in *The Heartbeat of Wounded Knee*, focusing on the massacres of Native Americans neglects the larger fact of the survivors. Treuer lays out a long triumphant saga of tribal activism and reclamation for the past 130 years. He's unequivocal in his prologue about the danger of highlighting atrocities. The book itself, he writes, stems from "the simple fierce conviction that our cultures are not dead and our civilizations have not been destroyed…I want to see Indian life as more than a legacy of loss and pain."

Plenty of fake or exaggerated massacres of Chinese Americans exist, too. Near Medical Springs, Oregon—south of Walla Walla, east of Hells Canyon—a wooden sign with white letters stood until a few years ago:

> *Lily White Mining Camp: A gold mining camp estab-*
> *lished in the 1860s and named after the wife of the camp*
> *boss. Population is said to have reached about 1000 souls*
> *including Chinese laborers. According to mint reports*
> *500,000 in gold was mined when the mines played out.*
> *An oft-told story relates that mine owners buried upwards*
> *of 100 Chinese men in a mine shaft rather than pay their*
> *wages.*

Historians are skeptical. If the Lily White Massacre happened, they ask, where is the corroborating information? Any of the following would help verify the legend, says scholar Priscilla Wegars: newspaper accounts, census records, archaeological remains, records of investigations by the Chinese government, or the hundred skeletons. (I can't resist a small rebuttal. They were supposedly buried in a mine shaft, so the skeletons would be awfully hard to find.) She notes in particular how rarely Chinese miners were "lode miners"; they placered down by the river, not up in the hills. (This argument applies to Chelan Falls, too. What were the miners doing up on the bluff?) Wegars's conclusion about the Lily White has a whiff of exasperation that transcends this one incident: "Such 'Chinese massacre' legends are common in mining country where the Chinese are known to have worked. It is true that many Chinese in the West were badly treated, and it is also true that some were murdered by Caucasians. However, unlike the 1887 Snake River Massacre [*sic*—the Hells Canyon Massacre] for which ample newspaper and other documentation exists, the supposed Lily White incident has no basis in fact."

Scholars have also aggressively debunked another would-be atrocity near Roslyn, Washington, the China Point Massacre. For 130 years, locals circulated stories of twenty-five Chinese men murdered in the late 1880s or maybe the 1870s. There's no clear date or location, and the perpetrators are described only as "cowboys." Nearly all accounts weave back to one first-person narrative published in 1954, written by Robert Bell, born in 1887, a man who would've been a toddler at the time of the supposed incident. Roslyn, later famous as the filming site for the TV show *Northern Exposure*, was a rough mining town. It had been the site of documented violence toward African American miners in the late 1880s. Matthew Hartman, who wrote an undergraduate thesis on the subject, posits that those stories got conflated with murders of Chinese miners. Like Wegars, he nods to the Hells Canyon Massacre as a possible seed source, and like Wegars, he advises caution: "The story should be viewed either as an amalgamation of other anti-Chinese hostilities or a myth designed to deter the Chinese from settling the region." Or to say it more plainly: "nothing more than a tale told by old-timers who enjoyed a good story."

Some stories go further, taking on a creepily campy tone. At a potluck in Stehekin, a friend told me one she'd heard from Bellingham. The coal mines, she said, tunneled under the bay had been worked mainly by Chinese men. When the mine was played out, the Chinese workers were either drowned or buried alive under the sea. I was saddened by the story—which I'd never heard—and unsurprised and by this point in my research, skeptical. Sure enough, a quick internet search unearthed a story that has circulated for more than a century in which six or (many) more Chinese workers were drowned or buried in an explosion in the Sehome Coal Mines in 1876. As with Chelan Falls, no primary sources exist from the era. Versions of the tale begin to appear in 1888 and grow increasingly sensational over time, suggesting that Chinese miners haunt caves under the city and/or that treasure lies just underground, and they culminate in a supposed curse on the town: either "once you arrive you will never leave" or "you will never escape." Few of the retellings mention the actual history: a total boycott of Chinese businesses turned to full-scale expulsion on November 5, 1885, when, according to historian Lottie Roth, "The thoroughly frightened Chinamen left the town as ordered, and their going was celebrated with a torchlight parade."

From the beginning, I was well aware the Chelan Falls Massacre may have been fabricated. Concie Luna, writing for *History Notes*, the newsletter of the Chelan County Historical Society in 2011, came to the conclusion nearly every other researcher had: something happened, but we don't know what. Her article is accompanied by a photo of rough buildings tucked against a dry hillside, with bowed rooflines "evocative of the curved roofs in China." Though the hillside does not seem to precisely match the steep bluffs near Beebe Bridge, the image is tantalizing enough to make me ache, a glimpse into a largely forgotten way of life.

Therein lies the rub. I'm haunted by the sobering possibility that erasing the massacres helps erase the Chinese people in the region from memory altogether. After all, the Chelan Falls Massacre is the only reason I started to learn about them. Without it, I'd never have heard of Chee Saw. The massacre was the shiny lure that hooked me. But that's no excuse to propagate a violent untruth, especially when, as Treuer argues so eloquently of Indigenous people, overstating the disappearance of the Chinese population undermines the experiences of Chinese Americans in the 150 years since. In *The Chinese Must Go*, Beth Lew-Williams argues similarly, "There are dangers to selectively shining the spotlight on moments when Chinese migrants were objects of white prejudice. Doing so reinforces the biases of the past and threatens to deprive the Chinese of their full humanity."

In his essay collection, *My Chinese America*, Allen Gee cheerfully bucks stereotypes. He's a Chinese American English professor—gifted at neither math nor music as Asian people are often presumed to be—a point guard, and an avid outdoorsman. He celebrates his own relative success while recounting the way his father was overlooked for promotions, and how Gee himself gets pulled over for driving-while-Asian. The title essay begins innocently with Gee's role as advisor to the Georgia College Bass Fishing Team, meanders through subheadings from all fifty states, and delves into darker territory including the fact that perpetrators of the Rock Springs Massacre were never prosecuted, but concludes with a celebration of Gee's literal and figurative mobility. He aspires to be a beacon for other immigrants looking to shed the kinds of expectations and limitations so-called history can exacerbate.

I sit at my desk too many hours a day: composing sentences, deleting them, and eventually, inevitably, hitting walls of ignorance and turning to the internet. Writers often describe research as "going down rabbit holes," as though the process is a pleasurable distraction, or a string of them, but getting lost in esoteric questions or chasing obscure facts leads eventually to questionable sources and begins to feel more like tunneling underground until next thing you know you're wading deep in sewer water. Google "Sandy Hook," for example, and you're three quick clicks away from an ugly conspiracy. Alex Jones, former host of Infowars, claimed "no one died" at Sandy Hook. He insisted the media fabricated the episode in order to promote stricter gun restrictions. Jones spread this horrifying ridiculousness until he had to submit to a deposition, and then he promptly backed off.

Only after he lost in court repeatedly to the families of children who died at Sandy Hook did he ascribe the conspiracy to "psychosis." Maybe he never believed his own lie. But if he didn't believe it, other people did. When the families sued Alex Jones, they were harassed, stalked, and threatened by his followers for years.

Which brings us to a crucial point about believing in made-up massacres: not believing in real ones is worse. As troubling as it may be to dredge up our violent past—real or imagined—deniers of atrocities have done far more damage with motives far more insidious. From the Holocaust to 9/11, "deniers" have fostered a dangerous debunking. In the case of the Holocaust, denying the gas chamber deaths of six million humans nurtures anti-Semitism as kindling for the next conflagration. In the case of Native Americans, denying the horrors allows the descendants and/or benefactors of those who stole land, killed women and children, and decimated species like the American bison in an effort to starve fellow humans to cleanse ourselves of guilt. And those are only the most widely known "denier" conspiracies.

In a 2015 article in the *Washington Post*, Adam Taylor outlines a dozen forgotten or downplayed massacres worldwide. Turkey denies the Armenian genocide. Japan downplays or ignores the Nanking Massacre in 1937 in which tens of thousands of Chinese people were killed. Until 2004, Germany refused to acknowledge the murders of over seventy-seven thousand Indigenous Herero and Namaqua people in Namibia. Russia still won't take responsibility for the Holodomor, in which over ten million people starved in a fake famine masterminded by Joséph Stalin. The list goes on and on.

There's a familiar dynamic at work, the myriad ways the powerful find to silence the powerless. Consider the #MeToo movement, police killing Black people, the unsolved murders of transgender and Indigenous women, generations of abused altar boys in Catholic churches. In every case, the weight of credulity leans hard toward the powerful, though they hardly need it. Who can hide evidence? Who can rewrite the report? Who can intimidate witnesses? Not the victims. For this reason, if there's any chance an atrocity occurred, we ought not dismiss it out of hand.

There was no holocaust of Chinese people in the West, but there was systematic oppression, a squeezing out. There were mass murders, some gruesome enough to earn the moniker of a massacre, and many smaller-scale events like the murder of hops pickers in the Squak Valley outside of Olympia, Washington. There was also the long chain of violent exclusions from Eureka, California, to Bellingham. By the mid-1880s "anti-Chinese violence became a vital expression of working class manliness," writes Beth Lew-Williams. Even as Chinese Americans acted with valiant resistance, the forces of tyranny accrued against them. About that, there's no titillating intrigue, no mystery, no doubt whatsoever.

Chapter Seventeen
AGAINST AMNESIA

onths passed during which life took me on a whirlwind of work, school, family, fancy. What seemed a novel adventure in Walla Walla had morphed into a lifestyle as new opportunities appeared, doors opened, and like so much of America, so much of the world, I was transported: alighted, alit, fleet-footed, on the road, in flight, from one side of the continent to the other. Until it stopped. News spread that a novel coronavirus had emerged, one the president insistently called the "China virus" or the "Wuhan virus." Within weeks, news reports accrued of Chinese Americans facing discrimination anew. The *New York Times* reported angry white people on the streets spitting on anyone who looked Asian. "It's you people who brought the disease," they cried. I found myself knocked off balance with shock and outrage. To understand xenophobia intellectually is one thing. To see it expressed so baldly, over and over, is unnerving.

In *America for Americans*, historian Erika Lee describes visiting Ellis Island in the days following the 2016 Republican National Convention where Donald Trump and others fanned the flames of immigrant-hate gleefully with falsehoods and exaggerations. Lee describes hearing the angry chants ("Build the wall! Build the wall!") and picturing the raised fists in her mind while taking in the gentle museum message: anti-immigrant history is over and done with. Lee knows the inspirational version of the immigrant-in-America story. Her grandparents, including one grandfather who slipped in with false papers and was detained under the Chinese Exclusion Act at Angel Island, worked hard as domestic servants, in restaurants, and in laundries to make the American Dream possible for their descendants. And it worked. A half century later, Lee is a professor of immigrant history at the University of Minnesota, an Andrew Carnegie fellow, a highly respected writer, and a public speaker in high demand. In *America for Americans*, she reminds readers that three-fifths of the world's immigrants landed in the United States between 1800 and 1900, and in the twentieth century we continued to accept more immigrants than any country on earth. But that doesn't mean everyone was welcomed with open arms. "Xenophobia has been neither an aberration nor a contradiction to the United States' history," Lee argues, but "a constant and defining feature of American life," one that's profitable for business and useful for calculating politicians. Her book tracks lesser-known stories of oppression by tracking the ways xenophobia initially aimed at European newcomers intensified when directed at non-white immigrants: Chinese, Japanese, Mexican, and Muslim. The stories surround us always and everywhere, but they're not always on the surface.

For many years, my friend Mandy Manning, the 2018 National Teacher of the Year, taught refugees in a "newcomers" class for high schoolers in Spokane that featured a flexible and wholly pragmatic curriculum covering necessary knowledge from language to technology to cultural norms. That's probably part of why she was chosen for the Teacher of the Year honor, as a rebuke to anti-immigrant policies, but since she stepped up, things had only gotten worse. When I went to visit her in fall of that year, I drove across Eastern Washington through a landscape scoured and shaped by an ice age eighteen thousand years ago, past fields where Mexican immigrants harvested crops, and I listened to an episode of *This American Life* recounting facts I'd known but could not digest. How the administration imposed a halt on refugees for 120 days then added a 90-day extension. How the number of nations from which immigrants are covered by Temporary Protected Status had been reduced by 98 percent. I hoped to meet some of her students.

When I showed up at Mandy's house, she was getting dressed and loudly expressing outrage. On her mantle sat a photo of her, her family, and the president of the United States at a White House ceremony to which she wore colorful buttons supporting rights for transgender people. Her hair, cut by a former student, shaved on one side, presented a challenge in itself to morning show TV hosts who could ask about little else. She's a mother, a stepmother, and former filmmaker who has taught in Texas and New York and who writes dazzling short stories with a darkly humorous feminist perspective. She had recently traveled to El Paso on Teacher of the Year business and passed the turnoff to the facility in Tornillo where immigrant children were being held, only a mile off the road, but when she asked to stop, her minders refused. They whisked her to the airport instead. When I arrived, Mandy was angry, still raging and organizing other teachers to go to Tornillo independently, to bring attention to the cause and to bring supplies as well, books in Spanish, anything, everything. Once she finished getting dressed, she announced we were off to visit not a student, but a colleague.

Luisa Orellana sat in her office at the community college where she teaches English as a second language, a slight, elegant woman taking time between classes to tell a story she'd told often. But not always. Not to everyone. She accepted my request for an interview only because Mandy vouched for me, and she began with her makeshift college education—before she had a green card, before she became a citizen—with evident delight.

In the late 1980s outside a university classroom, a woman sat alone writing in a notebook. The professor noticed but didn't speak to the woman. The next day, she appeared again. And the next. Luisa sat on a bench close enough to an open window to listen in. Finally one day, she waited at the doorway to ask about a particular assignment. What are you doing? the professor asked. She wanted to learn, Luisa said, but she couldn't sit in the class because, well, she couldn't. Within a couple of weeks, as the weather started to turn cold, one professor invited her in, and then another. For six years, this continued. A college education without the paper.

Luisa recalled these memories with pride, yes, but also intense gratitude, and this theme remained a through line as she traveled farther back in time. She came to the United States from El Salvador when she was eleven years old. Her family crossed through Guatemala and Mexico, landed in Hermosillo, in the Northern Mexican state of Sonora, south of Arizona. A priest there contacted the Presbyterian Church and members came for them—her mother with her nine children, Luisa among them, and three grandchildren—and two priests drove them to the border where volunteers stood on the other side awaiting them. The priests told them to run, and they did.

"We were taken into their arms," Luisa said.

"Did you feel like you were in danger?" I asked.

"I always felt that I was in danger."

In El Salvador, she explained, her father had been a deacon in the Catholic Church, one of the very first ordained because they didn't have enough priests in the poorer villages, and they needed someone to perform baptisms and marriages, so he was ordained and served more than 2,500 families. He'd travel to perform sacraments and to distribute powdered milk donated by aid agencies, but he also started groups to promote literacy and that was forbidden. He was close friends with Archbishop Oscar Romero, the Salvadoran bishop who was distrusted for his support of peasants, labeled a Marxist, and eventually assassinated in the middle of Sunday Mass. About a week after the assassination, Luisa's family got a late-night visit from a stranger who told them death squads were planning to come and burn down their house.

"He gave you warning?"

"Yes. We don't know why."

Her father knocked on the doors of all the people in the community, and everyone left in the night.

"There were so many miracles," Luisa said. "People don't believe in miracles, but there are so many things that make you wonder."

Her stories moved me. They chastised me, too. As Luisa Orellana insisted, an immigrant's story is richer and more complex, more filled with goodness than the oppression she overcame. The long tradition of people helping each other, newcomers especially, has deep roots in Chee Saw's saga, too. Wapato John packed supplies for his store. Chee Saw saved Dan Drumheller's cattle. Old Antoine, the formerly enslaved Black man, guarded the mouth of the Entiat for Chief Sil-so-saskt in exchange for a garden plot. Noah Brown stood up to defend Chinese neighbors even when he was outnumbered.

If we're going to tell stories of people who are gone and who left no record or none we've found yet, we'd best remember to never cast them as victims only. As I neared the end of writing this book, I gave a talk to writing students on the art of speculation, the ways we can imagine or color or recreate lives from the past on the page. Afterward, a student noted on the evaluation form the need to more fully address the complex ethical issues that arise when we do. Her criticism hit home. Should a person of the future—one from another country or, hell, another planet—try to describe what my life has been like, they'll likely get many or most things wrong. As I have with Chee Saw. On the other hand, to speculate is human. We do it all the time. Whether we voice it or not, we try to guess what others are thinking, what they've lived through, how they became who they are or who they seem to be. At its best, speculation is a way to tune our imaginations to empathy rather than exploitation, but, of course, even the most innocent speculation can turn to presumption. When given the opportunity to listen, we should.

Before I left, Luisa had one more story to tell. I'd switched off my recorder, but as she began to talk, Mandy urged me to turn it back on. Luisa began with some hesitation to describe an encounter that occurred recently with a woman she knew well at church.

When Luisa and her family first arrived in Spokane they'd been embraced by the community at St. Ann's Catholic Church. The parish was part of the Sanctuary Movement of the late 1980s—a web of church communities shielding undocumented people from persecution. Everyone at St. Ann's was supportive, or so Luisa always believed until this particular day. Luisa was walking out of church with this woman, and she wanted to acknowledge the kindnesses in the past. "I'll never forget what you did for us," Luisa said. "It was amazing that you risked your life. You could've been arrested." The woman's reply came as a surprise. "Well, I did help you," she said, "But I never agreed with it. I didn't want you to come here. We didn't want your family to come here."

"What did you say to that?" I asked.

"I was shocked. I said: 'I'm sorry. I didn't know you felt that way. I'm sorry you had to sacrifice yourself when you didn't agree. It's amazing. Not everyone does that.'"

"Maybe she didn't feel that way back then?" Mandy suggested.

Luisa shook her head. After this happened, this day at church, she explained, she decided to tell her family, and as she did, her brother-in-law almost started to cry. The woman had told him the same thing. She had told all Luisa's siblings.

"She made a point of telling everyone?" I said. "That is a hateful thing to do."

Mandy jumped in. "Isn't it? It's crazy."

On the recording for a few moments you no longer hear Luisa, only the two of us and our disgust, as Luisa tries to interrupt.

"That's not the end of the story," she said.

Just recently this woman stopped Luisa again. She said she'd decided she was glad the family landed in America, landed in the parish. She didn't exactly apologize, but she stepped back from her harsh words. This is what Luisa wants us to know, the note she wants to end on.

"It's hard to do something you don't want to do," Luisa said. "But she did it, and she did something good."

Any time you tackle xenophobia, you need to celebrate those who resisted and assisted ("Look for the helpers," as Mr. Rogers always said) by risking their safety, leaving water for those crossing a desert border or giving sanctuary to a family in a church community or organizing fellow teachers to draw attention to injustice and aid the imprisoned, and of course, you need to celebrate the immigrants themselves, so many of them. To be clear: Chinese Americans did not disappear from Washington State. Wing Chong Luke served as assistant attorney general from 1957-1962 and in 1962 was elected to Seattle City Council, the first Asian American to hold elected office in the state almost one hundred years after Chinese people outnumbered white people along the Columbia. Gary Locke, a third-generation Chinese American, served as governor from 1997 to 2005—the first person of Asian descent to be a governor in any of the lower forty-eight states—and was later tapped by President Obama to be secretary of commerce and ambassador to China. The list goes on.

Still, we ignore the undercurrent of hate at our own peril.

The photographer Haruka Sakaguchi started a project for *Time* magazine in early 2020 superimposing portraits of Asian Americans singled out for abuse during COVID-19 on photos of the locations where the interactions occurred. Her introduction traces the ties of disease and race hate in the United States. AIDS was blamed on Haitians, the 1918 "Spanish" flu was blamed on both the Spaniards and the Germans, the 2009 swine flu on Mexicans. Between March and July of 2020, she reports, more than 1,800 incidents of pandemic-fueled harassment or violence toward Asian Americans (or those who simply "look" Asian) had been reported in forty-five states, including many directed at medical workers. The encounters she reports are ugly and infuriating: a nurse shoved on the subway, a grocery patron intimidated out of the store, a young man cornered in a public restroom, to be coughed on and spit at. Her focus on minor transgressions, one after another after another, becomes an intentional subversion of scale. Virus-blaming is not the same as a lynching or a massacre. One danger of focusing only on extreme acts of xenophobia is to sensationalize violence. Another is to make microaggressions seem small beans—so unimportant as to be easily forgotten—when in fact they are the first early steps down a treacherous trail. What Sakaguchi with her Polaroid camera has done, alongside collaborator and writer Anna Purna Kambhampaty, is to force Americans to face a legacy many prefer to deny.

Erika Lee ends her introduction to *America for Americans* with a simple declarative message. "The history has been forgotten or erased, or taught to us as a series of mistakes. I am becoming convinced that this historical amnesia has left Americans ill-equipped to make sense of xenophobia today. Confronting the truth of this history is not enough to defeat xenophobia. But it is a start."

Chapter Eighteen
BONES

If one question haunts the story of the Chelan Falls Massacre more than any other, it's this: where are the bones? In the river, of course, people say. They sank to the bottom or washed out to sea, but this doesn't seem entirely credible. The bones of the victims of the Hells Canyon Massacre showed up more than thirty miles down the Snake River, according to a federal officer on the site, every one of them "shot, cut up, and stripped and thrown in the river." In a parallel and possibly conflated story, there are rumors of remains of the Chelan Falls Massacre victims showing up at Rock Island, thirty miles downriver, but the only date affixed to the rumor is 1868, seven years before the supposed massacre. (This could suggest, as Dorothy Petry's crystal swayed to attest, that Chinese people were murdered on more than one occasion along the Columbia.) Then there's the gruesome tale I'd heard from Sue Clouse about bodies floating up when Rocky Reach Dam caused the water level to rise in the 1960s, but if that happened, no physical evidence or written record remains. Maybe the bones simply disappeared. But that's unlikely.

To Chinese immigrants, bones mattered. A soul cannot rest, according to documents dating back to at least the Shang Dynasty (1600–1046 BCE), until the body returns to its native village, to its home. The widely held belief is expressed in a popular Cantonese saying: "Falling leaves return to their roots" (luo ye gui gen). Each year in China, and in places around the world where people of Chinese descent have settled permanently, families visit graves in celebration of Qingming or the Bright and Clear Day Festival in early April, a ritual tied to the fabric of life. They spend time with their ancestors, clean grave markers, and leave food and other gifts, material and symbolic, for the departed. At various times and places throughout history, they'd even dig up the bones themselves and clean them. In Chinese culture, care for bones is a deep spiritual practice, but to white people in the American West in the late nineteenth century and beyond, it seemed creepy or worse.

As much as the long braid or the slanted eyes, the strange diet or language, this idea of sending bones back home set Chinese immigrants apart and made them seem disloyal. This was not their home, obviously, if they'd spend good money to ship bones across the ocean. Some were required to pay fees, via the Sam Yup Benevolent Association or the Six Companies, for the reburial of their remains before they even left China. Some rich Chinese immigrants would even pay to hold a funeral for a family member on American soil and put the coffin in the ground, then pull the box back up and put it on the first boat back to China.

In these cases, in big cities like San Francisco, strict protocol had to be followed. All bodies were placed in lead or zinc coffins then encased in wood. A handbook from the Sam Yup Benevolent Association outlines exactly which parts must be collected when a body is dug up and/or reconstructed for transport, and it is nothing if not thorough.

Skull - one piece

Pigtail - one

Lower jaw - one

Cheek bones - one complete or three broken pieces

Chest bones - one complete or two broken pieces

Neck bones - 24 or more pieces

Ribs - nine to ten pieces on each side

Shoulder bones - 13 pieces on each side

Shoulder blades - one on each side

Upper limbs - Arms: 3 bones each side; Wrists: 8 small pieces each side; Hands: 19 pieces each side

Lower limbs - Hip: one bone each side; Legs: 3 on each side; Knee - one on each side; Ankles - 7 small pieces; Feet - 19 for each plus 3 small bean-like bones.

The list ends with an admonition: "Responsible supervisors and workers should follow this list, search carefully, and don't be casual about it. Be mindful, be mindful."

Most Chinese people in the Inland Northwest, miles from a big city, did not get fancy funerals. They lived and died hard, often too young and sadly. Most were men between twenty and fifty, and they died of tuberculosis, most often, and other diseases. They died of alcoholism and, some said, opium poisoning, though they usually smoked the drug, rather than injecting it, and it would take many pipes full to ingest a fatal dose. Chinese immigrants also had a very high rate of suicide, and often enough, homicide. But their bones were rarely neglected.

Some had prepaid for their bones to be brought home, but even if they did not, Chinese benefactors on both sides of the ocean donated money to retrieve their countrymen. Between 1874 and 1876, a society of men from Panyu, a region of Guangdong, collected money and hired a man named Yuet Chunk Paak to travel from San Francisco to British Columbia in search of the bodies of compatriots. When he found them, he followed the same protocols as were followed in the city. He placed the bones in metal boxes encased in wood, labeled with a name and a hometown. If no body or no complete body could be found, he had a procedure to follow.

"As for those who had perished in a watery grave," he wrote, "those who had been victims of foul play and whose bodies had been hidden in some secluded place, those whose bodies had been stolen by the white people to make fish bait, or those whose graves were missing markers and therefore unidentifiable, their names were inscribed on a silver plate, which was placed in a 'spirit' box and shipped back to the homeland."

In the end, Yuet Chunk Paak assembled 858 coffins and 24 spirit boxes and had them sent home at a cost of ten dollars each, and he was not the only one. In 1886, Hong Too, employed by the Sam Yup Benevolent Association, started a journey in Astoria, Oregon, and continued on to Portland and upriver to the Dalles. In 1896, another bone collector, Fang Chung, traveled from San Francisco to Washington, Idaho, and back, and retrieved more than 500 bodies.

Once the coffins and spirit boxes crossed the ocean, almost all ended up at the Tung Wah hospital in Hong Kong, which opened in 1872, where families could come retrieve them. Some bodies went unclaimed, but even these were cared for. A communal tomb existed at Chuangzhou Chest in Guangdong, and in 1893, 387 unclaimed bodies of gold miners who'd gone in search of Gold Mountain in America were buried in Renyu Tang cemetery in Xinhui province, each with its own epitaph.

There's another way bones matter to this story. In 1996, the remains of Kennewick Man were discovered a couple hundred miles south of Chelan Falls. White scientists lobbied for genetic testing and fought over his ancestry. Could this ten-thousand-year-old skeleton prove or disprove the ice-bridge theory of the settling of North America? Frankly, the Native people did not care. They were outraged at the exhumations and fought in the courts to rebury their ancestor, the one they came to call "the Ancient One." The Native American Graves Protection and Repatriation Act establishes tribal ownership of cultural items excavated or discovered on any federal or tribal land after November 16, 1990. But not on private lands. Native people persisted—their ancestors didn't recognize abstract lines on the land drawn by colonizers—and the bones of the Ancient One were reburied on February 18, 2017, with two hundred members of five Columbia Basin tribes in attendance at an undisclosed location.

If the Chinese miners had been disturbing graves, knowingly or unknowingly, digging where ancestors dwelled, this would have been no small offense. The strange detail of how the miners were attacked on a bluff rather than by the side of the river where placer mining takes place suggests they may have been prospecting with picks and shovels. Even if they were simply camping on the bluffs, they may have been digging where they oughtn't. White men would know the prohibition. If they wanted to blame Indigenous people, they'd have a motivation to assign: they were angry at the grave desecration.

For a long time, I held on to one thin sliver of hope. I believed it might be possible to find the remains of the victims of the Chelan Falls Massacre, however many or few there were, across the ocean. A traveling bone collector may have gathered their remains, I thought, and transported them home or recorded their names on a silver plate. This was hardly realistic. We don't know their names for one thing. The first recorded census from the region was in 1878, three years after the murders, and in all the census data from the era, Chinese populations are underrepresented for exactly the same reasons undocumented workers hesitate to talk to census workers today. Moreover, as many skeptical scholars had pointed out to me, the Chinese government kept track of sojourners to "Gold Mountain." They would have intervened if even a small number went missing. Still, I held on to hope that someone from a small village in Guangdong might someday get in touch out of the blue.

*

Dr. Raymond Chong emailed me in April 2021. He had found a short essay I wrote about the massacre online, and he wanted to know more. An engineer by trade, he was working in his spare time to educate Americans about mistreatment of Chinese Americans. He'd written about Rock Springs, about Hells Canyon, and couldn't believe he'd never heard about Chelan Falls. When we spoke on the phone, he told me more of his personal story. He'd grown up in Los Angeles, near Chinatown, eating Cantonese cuisine and celebrating traditional festivals, but he was, according to his website, a "jook sing," a bamboo rod: Chinese on the outside, American on the inside. Solid on the outside, and hollow within.

In 2003, after a personal tragedy—a friend's suicide—he grew interested in tracing his roots. He traveled to his ancestral village, Long Gang Li, in Kaiping County, in Guangdong, a "poor village in dilapidated condition" where he found members of the Zhang clan waiting for him. They'd built a modest home with money his great-grandfather made as an opium purveyor and gambling lord in Boston, and they said they'd been waiting for Ray to return. In 2008, he returned once more and together with fifty members of the Zhang clan hiked through a eucalyptus forest to pay respects to his ancestors.

Ray's warmth and his commitment to unburying history made him an instant ally. He collated the articles available online as well as those I'd collected, hard copy, from archives. He recruited his brother, a dogged researcher, who took up the cause with vigor and made GPS maps showing any bluff three hundred feet above the river. (Exactly as we'd supposed, the only ones were along the Chelan River, not the Columbia.) He contacted relatives in Guangdong…who knew nothing.

Ray Chong also introduced me, via email, to two archaeologists, Eric Gleason and Jacqui Cheung, who had recently become interested in the story. Eric and Jacqui had stumbled upon their own treasure trove of Chinese history in the Pacific Northwest when they bought an old brick building in The Dalles, Oregon, and began excavating for a new deck only to discover a trash pit in the backyard that had been used from 1879 to 1950 and contained boxes and boxes of Chinese artifacts, evidence of lives rarely acknowledged, stories rarely told. They'd looked into the Chelan Falls Massacre for a conference presentation, trekked through many of the same sources I'd found, and come to the same non-conclusions. They also worked for the Colville federated tribes, and when they asked their colleagues about the massacre, found that they, too, were skeptical. The US Army, led by Major General Oliver Otis Howard, would have been keeping close tabs on the region, they said, yet Howard's extensive memoirs mention nothing of the event.

The chorus was growing louder: the massacre did not happen.

"With no documented protest by the Chinese consul general," Ray Chong insisted, "there was no massacre, but perhaps several killings by whites that triggered the Chinese gold miners to flee for their lives."

Why, then, I asked him, did the story persist?

"The white power structure would have seized the grand opportunity to demonize the heathen Chinese and savage Indians. A perfect way to attack both non-white peoples and to further scare away Chinese immigration."

I asked Eric Gleason the same question, why a massacre might be made up. "I do think some of it is connected to anti-Chinese exclusion," he wrote, "and increasing settlement and development. Settlers were beginning to write about themselves as tamers of the land and the Wild West, patting themselves on the back for all the progress and improvements they have made, and likely looking for investors."

He quoted lines that had stood out to me, too, from Richard Steele. "Now the placer fields of the past are owned by settlers, and are fast becoming beautiful orchards…" A sales pitch if you've ever heard one.

Eric and Jacqui weren't quite as quick to give up the ghost as Ray Chong. Eric noted that more work had recently been done at Beebe Bridge Park to rebuild a boat launch and he'd heard rumor that Chinese artifacts had been found. He said he would keep me posted. Still, the chance that these "artifacts" are bones remains extremely remote.

As for any would-be perpetrators, their bones would be easier to find. The Manson Cemetery is home to several Chelans, including fourteen who were buried near Chelan Falls in 1887 and dug up during a construction project in 1985 and moved. The Chelan Cemetery is home to early white settlers like Lewis Woodin, who built the first lumber mill in Chelan, and Noah N. Brown, who stood up against the Chinese exclusion law in Wenatchee, among others. Their lives, meanwhile, exist only in hearsay and guesses. They bragged in a corner tavern or took the secret to the grave. They sired children or lost them to violence or sickness. They bought swaths of land, opened mines, marveled at the sunrise, played music, picked meat from the bones of animals we see less and less frequently these days: bighorn sheep, elk, mountain goats. They built hotels or followed gold up the Yukon or logged trees on the Colville Reservation. Then they died.

As for Chee Saw, I believe his bones stayed somewhere in the Columbia River watershed where Dorothy Petry placed them near Myers Creek or elsewhere on Gold Mountain. Not all Chinese American bones crossed the ocean. The Mountain View Cemetery in Walla Walla, for example, contains more than seventy Chinese American graves dating back to 1909. Historians speculate that "a small city distant from the major Chinese population centers lacked the usual sojourners' institutions charged with ensuring that the dead, after a suitable time in an American grave, would be dug up again and sent to China." If Walla Walla is small, Chelan Falls is smaller, and Chesaw is miniscule.

But the reason I want to believe his bones stayed doesn't lie in geography or expediency or finances. Chee Saw stayed in the Upper Columbia for his entire adult life. He survived economic unrest and a maybe massacre, the arrival of Miller's store, steamships and railroads. He grubstaked claims, rustled cattle, ferried rapids in a rowboat, crisscrossed an international border as a smuggler or a renegade, and made a good name for himself. "Chee Saw," they say, meant a "good deal." He married and raised children. He made this place his home. This land of contradictions—of deserts carved by rivers and hills of endless golden light, but precious little actual gold—is where he'd choose to have his bones stay.

Another interpretation of the Chinese belief system is that bones must be returned home so the spirits of the dead can protect the living. When I consider the deep comfort this must bring, to know with certainty your ancestors watch over you, I feel displacement like a loss. This is the choice I made by leaving my childhood home, the same choice my parents made and their parents made and their parents, too. As COVID-19 raged, freezer trucks lined up outside hospitals, and mass graves were dug, I prepared to leave for another job, pandemic be damned. The instinct to move is apparently as hardwired in me as in salmon or butterflies or birds. Even so, when the time comes, I want my remains to bleed gray into a blue-green torrent beneath a high bridge. Moving water, more than dirt, is my home. This much I share with all people who've passed this way: one river, moving steady, from the summer snowy peaks to the sea.

In "The Ghosts of Bitter Creek," Teow Lim Goh describes writing about the Rock Springs Massacre. "I don't believe in ghosts," she writes, "but as I worked on these poems, I felt another kind of presence—the people who are not represented in the archives." I feel this presence, too, and with it a responsibility. I've contacted Chee Saw's descendants, or people who may be his descendants, on the Colville Reservation, in Osoyoos and Alberta, and beyond. If they are children of his children's children, they do not know it. They've never heard of him, but they're curious to learn.

So I end where I began, where ancestry wears a different coat. Not blood, but place. Not fixed, but in flux. If the dead can protect the living, we owe a debt to the dead, too: to reimagine their lives, to recognize our kinship, to share stories and learn hard lessons even from half-truths and lies, and always, as best we can, to treat the fragments with care.

References

Bailey, Jim. "The Coming of the Chinese: Strangers on the Land," Keynote address, Lake Chelan Historical Society Meeting, April 16, 1984.

Banse, Tom. "Fixer-Upper in the Dalles Yields Valuable Chinese Artifacts." Aired July 6, 2011 on National Public Radio.

Bodmer, Miles and Doug Toomey. "Where the Pacific Northwest's Big One is Most Likely to Strike." *Scientific American*, Aug. 5, 2018.

Borg, Ted. "The China Ditch: Fountainhead for Gold and Apples." *Okanogan County Heritage*, Fall 1986.

Bronson, Ben. Email to Ana Maria Spagna, Gregory Nokes, Marcus Less, Chuimei Ho. Subject line: "The Chelan Massacre." Nov. 7, 2017.

Caudell, Justus. "Wenatchi Hold Membership Meeting." *Tribal Tribune*, April 27, 2018.

Cebula, Larry. *Plateau Indians and the Quest for Spiritual Power, 1700-1850*. Lincoln: University of Nebraska Press, 2003.

Chan, Jeffrey Paul, Frank Chin, Lawson Fusao Inada, and Shawn Wong, eds. *The Big Aiiieeeee!: An Anthology of Chinese American and Japanese American Literature*. New York: Meridian Books, 1991.

Chelan Falls Leader. "Early Days on the River - Lively Tale of Chinese Gold Hunters." June 2, 1892.

Chin, Art and Doug. "The Chinese in Washington State." *News* (blog), *OCA Greater Seattle*, 2013. https://ocaseattle.org/2013/05/13/chinese-in-washington-state/

Chin, Art. *Golden Tassels: A History of the Chinese in Washington 1857-*

1977. Self-published, Seattle, WA, 1977.

Chong, Raymond. "The Zhang Clan Odyssey." https://www.mychina-roots.com/samples/zhang-odyssey/index. html#140

--- Email correspondence to Ana Maria Spagna, Jaqui Cheung, and Eric Gleason. Subject line "Chelan Fall Massacre – Data." May 12, 2021.

Chung, Sue Fawn and Priscilla Wegars. *Chinese American Death Rituals: Respecting the Ancestors*. Lanham: Altamira Press, 2005.

Chung, Sue Fawn. *In Pursuit of Gold: Chinese American Miners and Merchants in the American West*. Urbana: University of Illinois Press, 2011.

CINARC. "The Chelan Massacre Reconsidered." Updated August 30, 2018. https://www.cinarc.org/Violence-2.htm- l#anchor_162

Davis, George. "Where Yellow Men Sought Yellow Metal." *Okanogan County Heritage*, Spring 1976.

Deseret News. "Idaho Legend's Days May be Numbered." Jan. 18, 1994.

Drumheller, Dan. "Uncle Dan Drumheller Tells Thrills of Western Trails in 1854." Fairfield, WA: Ye Galleon Press, 1985.

Downing, Alfred. "A Trip to Lake Chelan" *Stehekin: Glimpses of the Past: A Collection of Early Writings*. Edited by Carol Stone. Friday Harbor, WA: Long House Printcrafters and Publishers, 1983.

Esvelt, John. "Upper Columbia Chinese Placering." *The Pacific Northwesterner* 3, no. 1. (Winter, 1959).

Esvelt, John. "Chinese Placer Mining on the Upper Columbia." Unpublished manuscript. Spokane Public Library, 1954.

Evening Statesmen. "A Peculiar Case in Criminal Court: For a Consideration One Chinaman Confesses Murder Committed by Another." July 31, 1903.

Evenson, Lindsey M. "Pre-1900s Chinese Placer Mining in Northeastern Washington State: An Archeological Investigation." MA thesis, Eastern Washington University, 2016.

Fries, U.E. *From Copenhagen to Okanogan: The Autobiography of a Pioneer*. Portland: Binford & Mort Publishing, 1984.

Gaylord, Mary. *Eastern Washington's Past: Chinese & Other Pioneers:*

1860-1910. D.C.: Forest Service USDA, 1993.

Gee, Allen. *My Chinese-America.* Santa Fe: Santa Fe Writers Project, 2015.

Gleason, Eric, and Jacqueline Cheung. "Revisiting the Chinese Store Near Chelan Falls, Washington and the 1875 Massacre of Chinese Miners." Presented at the Northwest Anthropological Conference, April 2021.

Goh, Teow Lim. "Chinatown Burning." In *The Georgia Review*, forthcoming, and *Bitter Creek*, an unpublished manuscript.

––– "The Ghosts of Bitter Creek" in *Western Journeys.* Salt Lake City: University of Utah Press, 2022.

Hackenmiller, Tom. *Wapato Heritage: The History of Chelan and Entiat Indians.* Manson: Point Publishing, 1995.

Hartman, Michael. "A Massacre at China Point." An undergraduate thesis, University of Washington Tacoma, 2015.

Herald Reporter. "Pioneer Accounts of Early Pateros." Dec. 15, 1960.

Hildebrand, Lorraine Barker. *Straw Hats, Sandals and Steel: The Chinese in Washington State.* Tacoma: The WA State American Revolution Bicentennial Commission, 1977.

History (*website*). "Soldiers Massacre Sleeping Camp of Native Americans." This Day in History, January 23. Updated January 20, 2022. https://www.history.com/this-day-in-history/soldiers-massacre-the-wrong-camp-of-indians.

Ho, Chuimei and Bennet Bronson. "The Chelan Massacre Reconsidered" April 21, 2013 https://www.cinarc.org/Violence-2.html#anchor_162

Hodgen, D. "River Steamers Brought Early Settlers to Pateros." *Okanogan Independent.* 1927.

Howard, Oliver Otis. *My Life and Experiences Among Our Hostile Indians.* Boston: DeCapo Press, 1972.

Horwitz, Tony. "Horrific Sand Creek Massacre Will be Forgotten No More." *Smithsonian*, December 2014.

Horowitz, Donald L. *Ethnic Groups in Conflict.* Berkeley: University of California Press, 1985.

Kearney, Dennis and H. L. Knight. "Appeal from California. The Chinese Invasion. Workingmen's Address." *Indianapolis Times*, February 28, 1878.

LaBree, Kolby. "The Chinese Curse of Bad Town: Episode 2," *The City of Subdued Podcast*, Oct. 12, 2020. Podcast, website, 24:37. https://bellinghistory.com/blog/2020/10/13/the-chinese-curse-of-bad-town-episode-2

Layman, William. *Native River: the Columbia Remembered*. Pullman: Washington State University Press, 2002.

Lee, Erika. *America for Americans: A History of Xenophobia in the United States*. New York: Basic Books, 2020.

Lew-Williams, Beth. *The Chinese Must Go: Violence, Exclusion, and the Making of the Alien in America*. Cambridge: Harvard University Press, 2018.

Liestman, Daniel. "Horizontal Inter-ethnic Relations: Chinese and American Indians in Nineteenth-Century American West." *Western Historical Quarterly* 30, no. 3, August 1, 1999.

Luna, Concie. "A Chinese Puzzle." *History Notes: Newsletter of the Chelan Historical Society*, 2011.

Majors, Harry M., Ed. *Northwest Discovery: The Journal of Northwest History and Natural History* 4 no 1. (June 1983): "Downing's Misadventure on the Columbia River" "Backus Explores the Twisp and Methow Valleys."

Marchand, Arnie. *"The Way I Heard It" A Three Nation Reading Vacation*. Oroville, Washington: Heritage Productions, 2013.

–––Interview with the author, May 14, 2019.

Martin, Ken and Vida. "The Poland-China Mine." In *Gold Mining in Washington State: Yesterday and Today*. Bentonville: Gold Treasures Publishing, 1995.

Mather, Ken. *Frontier Cowboys and the Great Divide: Early Ranching in BC and Alberta*. Canada: Heritage House Publishing Company, Ltd., 1947.

Matthews, Mychel. "Fake Massacre and Wagon Trails: Almo's History." *MagicValley.com* Updated October 20, 2013. https://magicvalley.com/news/local/fake-massacre-and-wagon-trails-almos-history/

article_90347e4b-fda5-509c-a87d-bd4374ddd6fb.html

McDonald, Lucile. "Old Mine Town Named for Chinese." *Seattle Daily Times*, November 27, 1960.

McGrath, Marjorie Pattie. *Pioneer in Pigtails: A Sketch of the Earlier Days in Douglas County*. Self-published, 1985.

McMurtry, Larry. *Oh What a Slaughter: Massacres in the American West 1846-1890*. New York: Simon & Schuster, 2005.

Mierendorff, Bob. Email to Ana Maria Spagna. Subject line: "1892 article." Nov. 16, 2018.

Miller, Sam. Store ledgers. Wenatchee Valley Museum and Cultural Center archives.

Molzhan, Rod. "Long Jim, the Last Chief of the Chelans." *The Good Life* (blog). May 28, 2019. https://bloggingthegoodlife.com/articles/columnist-articles/long-jim-last-chief-of-the-chelans/

Mourning Dove. *A Salishan Autobiography*. Lincoln: University of Nebraska Press, 1990.

National Park Service *(website)*. "Sand Creek Massacre." History & Culture. Updated June 25, 2020. https://www.nps.gov/sand/ learn/historyculture/index.htm.

Nelson, Judy. "The Final Journey Home: Chinese Burial Practices in Spokane." *Pacific Northwest Forum* 6, no. 1 (1993): 70-76.

Nestertoff, Greg. "Chinese Canadian Births at Rock Creek." *The Kütney Reader* (blog). June 11, 2018. https://gregnesteroff.wixsite.com/kutnereader/post/chinese-canadian-and-indigenous-births-at-rock-creek

Nokes, R. Gregory. *Massacred for Gold: The Chinese in Hells Canyon*. Corvallis: Oregon State University Press, 2009.

Okanogan County Heritage. "I Don't Remember Joe Chesaw's Father…" 1973.

Olzak, Susan. *The Dynamics of Ethnic Competition and Conflict*. Redwood City: Stanford UP, 1992.

Omak Chronicle. "Chee Saw Was Unique Figure in the Highlands." August 7, 1969.

Orellana, Luisa. Interview with the author. Oct. 4, 2018.

Pasley, Thomas. "Placering at Pateros." *Okanogan County Heritage*, Fall 1974.

Pettit, Stephanie. "Slaughter of Horses Leaves Lasting Mark." *Spokesman-Review*, Oct. 1, 2009.

Rader, Chris. "Chinese Mined Around Wenatchee." *Confluence: Publication of the Wenatchee Valley Museum & Cultural Center* 28, No. 4. (Winter 2012-13).

Ramsey, Guy Reed. *Postmarked Washington Okanogan County*. Fairfield, WA: Ye Galleon Press, 1977.

Ruby, Robert H. and John A. Brown. *Half-Sun on the Columbia: A Biography of Chief Moses*. Norman: University of Oklahoma Press, 1995.

Sakaguchi, Haruka and Anna Purna Kambhampaty. "I Will Not Stand Silent: 10 Asian Americans Reflect on Racism During the Pandemic and the Need for Equality." Time, June 25, 2020.

Scheurman, Richard D. *The Wenatchi Indians: Guardians of the Valley*. Fairfield, WA: Ye Galleon Press, 1982.

Seattle Post-Intelligencer "The Isle of Lepers: A New Molokai for Victoria's Rotting Chinamen." May 26, 1891.

Simmons, Kim A., Mary P. Rossillon and Randal F. Schalk. *A Cultural Resource Survey of "Exhibit R" Recreation Sites in the Rocky Reach Reservoir*. Project Report Number 16, Laboratory of Archaeology and History, Washington State University, 1983.

Simmons, Kim. Phone interview with the author. April 8, 2019.

Smith, Hoke and George Shaw. Transcription of a reel-to-reel tape owned by Okanogan County Historical Society. March 11, 1965.

Splawn A.J. *Ka-Mi-Akin: Last Hero of the Yakimas*. Caldwell, ID: *The Caxton Printers*, 1917.

Spokane Falls Review, "The Chelan Indians – A Spirited Statement by Responsible Citizens." January 8, 1891.

Spokesman. "Heathen Pioneers." May 19, 1892.

Stamper, Marcy "High Hopes and Deep Snows, How Mining Spurred Development of the Methow Valley," Winthrop: Shafer Historical Museum.

Steele, Richard F. *An Illustrated History of Stevens, Ferry, Okanogan and Chelan Counties.* Spokane: Western Historical Publishing Company, 1904.

Tavernise, Sabrina and Richard A. Oppel, Jr. "Spit on, Yelled At, Attacked: Chinese-Americans Fear for Their Safety." *New York Times*, March 23, 2020.

Toone, Trent. "Because it's Sacred Land: Shoshone Nation Chairman is on a Mission to Share Massacre Site with World." *Deseret News*, Sept. 9, 2018.

Taylor, Adam. "It Wasn't Just the Armenians: Other 20th Century Massacres We Ignore." *The Washington Post,* April 24, 2015.

Treuer, David. *The Heartbeat of Wounded Knee: Native America from 1890 to the Present.* New York: Riverhead, 2019.

Walla Walla Union Bulletin. "Old Mining Town, Ghost of Its Former Self, Turns 100." June 1, 1998.

Wegars, Priscilla, ed. *Hidden Heritage: Historical Archeology of the Overseas Chinese.* Amityville: Baywood Publishing, 1993.

Wegars, Priscilla. Comments on the Lily White Massacre, November 26, 2010. https://www.cinarc.org/Violence.htm- l#anchor_224

Wellman, Candace. *Peace Weavers: Uniting the Salish Coat Through Cross-Cultural Marriages.* Pullman: Washington State University Press, 2017.

Wenatchee World. "Chelan area. W.T. – on Wapato John." Feb. 17, 1972.

Wenatchee World, "Early History Reads Like Romance." Dec. 22, 1910.

Wenatchee World. "Gold Eludes Chinaman." March 17, 1926.

Wenatchee Daily World. "Ribbon Cliff Monster Worried the Indians." July 30, 1932.

Wilma, David. "Chelan County – Thumbnail History." January 26, 2006. http://www.historylink.org/File/7624 Wilson, Bruce A. *Late Frontier: A History of Okanogan County, Washington.* Okanogan: Okanogan Historical Society, 1990.

Wong Sam and Assistants, *An English-Chinese Phrase Book.* San Francisco: Cubery & Co., 1875.

Woodhouse, Philip R., Daryl Jacobsen, & Victor Pisoni. *Discovering*

Washington's Historic Mines: Volume 4: The Western Okanogan. Monroe, WA: Northwest Mining Publishers, 2011.

Yung, Judy, Gordon H. Chang and Him Mark Lai. *Chinese American Voices: From the Gold Rush to the Present.* Berkeley: University of California Press, 2006.

Zhu, Liping. "No Need to Rush: The Chinese, Placer Mining, and the Western Environment." *Montana: The Magazine of Western History* 49, no. 3 (Autumn 1999).

Acknowledgments

This project has been a journey, and I owe gratitude to those who helped.

My sincere thanks…

To Washington State Artist Trust Grants for Artists Program for support of the research and writing of this book and to *Fourth Genre: Explorations in Nonfiction* for publishing an excerpt titled "Massacre" in Issue 22.1 Spring 2020. To friends old and new who joined me on jaunts around the region: Sue and Dave Clouse, Larry Cebula, Bill Layman, Randy Lewis (K'ayaxan), Mandy Manning, and Luisa Orellana. To the kind and dedicated volunteers at Okanogan Borderlands Historical Society in Oroville, Washington: Dorothy Petry, Ellen Barttels, Kay and Mike Sibley, and Arnie Marchand. To the fabulous Fairfield workshop crew Carlye Mazzucco, Kristen Dalli, Emily Dillon, Barb Chintz and our dear mentors, Lynn Strong, Adriana Páramo, Eugenia Kim, Sonya Huber, and Carol Ann Davis for invaluable feedback and camaraderie. To Laura Pritchett and Chris LaTray for reading the draft manuscript and offering smart and useful suggestions. Every writer should have such generous friends. To the researchers, writers, tribal members, and scholars who informed my thinking: Allen Gee, Gregory Nokes, Chuimei Ho, Ben Bronson, Art Chin, Priscilla Wegars, Teow Lim Goh, Marcy Stamper, Richard Hart, Drew Wilson, and so many others. To archaeologists Bob Mierendorf, Eric Gleason, Jacqui Cheung, and Kim Simmons for your stories, knowledge, expertise, and willingness to correspond ... and to speculate. To Alya Bohr for research assistance, patience, and keen eyesight. To Keith Carpenter, Monica Libbey, and the crew for welcoming me in the orchard. To Dr. Raymond Chong for his deep commitment to history and to the truth.

And to Laurie, always.

About the Author

Ana Maria Spagna is the author of nine books including the young adult novel *The Luckiest Scar on Earth* and most recently the poetry chapbook *Mile Marker Six*. Her work has been recognized by the River Teeth Literary Nonfiction Prize, the Society for Environmental Journalists, the Nautilus Book Awards, and as a four-time finalist for the Washington State Book Award. A former backcountry trails worker, Ana Maria now teaches in MFA programs at Antioch University Los Angeles, Western Colorado University, and St. Lawrence University.

Torrey House Press

Voices for the Land

The economy is a wholly owned subsidiary of the environment, not the other way around.
—Senator Gaylord Nelson, founder of Earth Day

Torrey House Press publishes books at the intersection of the literary arts and environmental advocacy. THP authors explore the diversity of human experiences with the environment and engage community in conversations about landscape, literature, and the future of our ever-changing planet, inspiring action toward a more just world. We believe that lively, contemporary literature is at the cutting edge of social change. We seek to inform, expand, and reshape the dialogue on environmental justice and stewardship for the human and more-than-human world by elevating literary excellence from diverse voices.

Visit www.torreyhouse.org for reading group discussion guides, author interviews, and more.

As a 501(c)(3) nonprofit publisher, our work is made possible by generous donations from readers like you.

Torrey House Press is supported by Back of Beyond Books, the King's English Bookshop, Maria's Bookshop, the Jeffrey S. & Helen H. Cardon Foundation, the Diane & Sam Stewart Family Foundation, the Barker Foundation, the George S. & Dolores Doré Eccles Foundation, Diana Allison, Klaus Bielefeldt, Laurie Hilyer, Kitty Swenson, Shelby Tisdale, Kirtly Parker Jones, Robert Aagard & Camille Bailey Aagard, Kif Augustine Adams & Stirling Adams, Rose Chilcoat & Mark Franklin, Linc Cornell & Lois Cornell, Susan Cushman & Charlie Quimby, Betsy Gaines Quammen & David Quammen, the Utah Division of Arts & Museums, Utah Humanities, the National Endowment for the Humanities, the National Endowment for the Arts, the Salt Lake City Arts Council, the Utah Governor's Office of Economic Development, and Salt Lake County Zoo, Arts & Parks. Our thanks to individual donors, members, and the Torrey House Press board of directors for their valued support.

Join the Torrey House Press family and give today at www.torreyhouse.org/give.